MONTAGNAIS

SAULTEAUX

*Hiawatha is described as
an Iroquois by Longfellow,
but Indian Legends make
him belong to the Ojibway.*

MALECITE
PASSAMAQUODDY

OJIBWAY
(CHIPPEWA)

SIOUX

OTTAWA ▲

ABNAKI ▲   PENOBSCOT

ALGONQUIN ▲

MENOMINI
WINNEBAGO ▲
SAC-FOX

PENNACOOK ▲

CHIPPEWA

HURON
TUSCARORA

LONG HOUSE
IROQUOIS
(Cayuga, Oneida, Mohawk,
Onondaga, Seneca, Tuscarora)

MASSACHUSETTS
PEQUOT
WAMPANOAG

POTAWATOMI

PIANKASHAW

WYANDOT ▲

NARRAGANSET

IOWA ▲

MIAMI

KICKAPOO ▲

NEUTRALS ▲
ERIE

DELAWARE ▲

JOHN ELIOT 1604-1690.
First missionary to
the Indians

ROGER WILLIAMS.
1604-1684
Preached to Wampanoag
and Narraganset tribes

ILLINOIS

SUSQUEHANNA

PAMUNKEY

NANTICOKE ▲

JAMESTOWN, founded in 1607
First permanent English
settlement in America. · · ·
Here Pocahontas, daughter of
Powhatan, married John
Rolfe.

OSAGE

SHAWNEE

CHICKAHOMINY

QUAPAW

TUTELO ▲
TUSCARORA ▲

CATAWBA

LOCATED IN OKLAHOMA:
· OTTAWA · QUAPAW · PEORIA
·EE · WYANDOT · SAC & FOX
·WATOMI · CHEROKEE · OSAGE
· TONKAWA · PAWNEE
·OO · DELAWARE · WICHITA
·ANCHE · APACHE · IOWA
·KASAW · CHOCTAW · CREEK

UPPER CREEK

SEQUOYAH 1760-1843
Devised first Indian
alphabet and taught
Cherokees to read and
write.

YUCHI

CHICKASAW

CHOCTAW

CADDO ▲

TUNICAN

LOWER CREEK

NATCHEZ

ALIBAMU

CHITIMACHA

APALACHEE

SEMINOLE

TIMUQUANAN

INDIANS
OF THE
U·S·A·

▲ SYMBOL SHOWS HISTORIC
LOCATION OF TRIBES NOW
LIVING, IN WHOLE, OR IN PART,
IN OTHER AREAS.

INDIANS
ARE PEOPLE, TOO

BY

RUTH MUSKRAT BRONSON

FRIENDSHIP PRESS
NEW YORK

RUTH MUSKRAT BRONSON is a native of Oklahoma. Her father is a Cherokee Indian who was born in those tragic times when the "Trail of Tears" was a vivid and recent memory. After completing work in the public schools of her state, she attended the University of Kansas, where she had an opportunity to serve as student counselor at the Methodist Home for Indian Girls at Lawrence. Later she was graduated from Mt. Holyoke College and did graduate study at George Washington University in Washington, D. C. In 1922 she was sent as a delegate representing the Indian students in the United States to the World's Student Christian Federation Conference in Peking, China. In 1925 she entered the service of the Office of Indian Affairs of the Department of the Interior of the United States. She was first a teacher of English at Haskell Institute in Lawrence, Kansas, and then was assigned to do guidance and placement work for the Indian Service, with headquarters in Kansas City, Missouri. In 1931 she became Guidance Officer for the entire Indian Service, a position that she held for more than twelve years. During this period her responsibilities were administering an educational student loan fund for Indian students, counseling Indian students in institutions of higher learning, and establishing contacts with organizations interested in giving scholarships to Indian students. In 1928 she was married to John F. Bronson of Beacon Falls, Connecticut. Her home today is in Washington, D. C.

Cover design by MARY SULLY

To

MRS. FRED S. BENNETT

*in deep appreciation of her devoted service
to my people*

CONTENTS

CHAPTER FIVE

WHO SHALL LEAD THE PEOPLE?   127

1: WARDS IN THE HOMELAND

> We hold these truths to be self-evident, that all men
> are created equal, that they are endowed by their
> Creator with certain unalienable Rights, that among
> these are Life, Liberty, and the pursuit of Happiness.

A FEW years ago an Indian student was asked
to interpret his people to a conference of educational advisers.

"I am an Indian," he told them. "I am proud of it.
. . . The same God who created the heavens and earth
created both you and me in his likeness. I have a heart,
just the same as yours. My soul is just as acceptable to
God as yours. True, my skin may be a shade darker than
yours, but does that matter? What really counts is the
kind of persons we are, you and I. I have heartaches,
just the same as you do. I have joys, pleasures, ambitions,
griefs, sorrows, and disappointments. So do you. I love
my home and people just the same as you do—I am an
American. I am an Indian." [1]

So might any Indian from any tribe in America speak
for his people to an alien group. So, also, might you or I
seek the understanding of people to whom we are un-

[1] Harvey Allison in *Indians at Work*, July, 1936.

known. Hiamovi, chief of the Cheyennes, who lived long ago, expressed the same idea in different language:

"There are birds of many colors—red, blue, green, yellow—yet all one bird. There are horses of many colors—brown, black, yellow, white—yet all one horse. So cattle; so all living things—animals, flowers, trees. So men; in this land where once were only Indians are now men of every color—white, black, yellow, red—yet all one people."

Most people who do not know Indians well think of them as strange and inscrutable. So much confusion and sentimentality have been added to our superficial impressions that it is difficult to allow Indians human qualities of strength and weakness like our own. Yet what Indians want most is for us to remember that they, too, are persons like ourselves, subject to the same psychological laws governing all human beings; touched by the same kindnesses as others; shaped and molded by the things that have happened to them over the years, just as we are patterned by our experiences. Our failure to apply this principle in our dealings with Indians has always resulted in increased difficulties for them.

A STRONG AND POWERFUL PEOPLE

There are some thirty million Indians living in the Western hemisphere, scattered across the two continents from Alaska to Cape Horn. Here is a race of people powerful enough in numbers alone to wield profound influence on the future of the world. The slow centuries, freighted with tragedy for Indians, have established for them the right to consider themselves a strong and great people. They were adventurous enough, back when the world was new, to leave their Asiatic home and to journey across a dark and unknown land. They were brave enough to venture into the New World, defenseless against the uncertain terrors of ice and wilderness save for tools carved only with their bare hands. And they have been strong enough to endure captivity and degradation through generations and to emerge, in our time, from their grim twilight with spirit unbroken.

In the United States there are today approximately 376,000 Indians.[1] Many of this number are only part Indian for, like all races, Indians have intermingled with other people with whom the group has come in contact. Patiently, stubbornly, and with unimaginable suffering, these original inhabitants of our country have kept their tenuous hold on the life of this nation, refusing to be destroyed; refusing, for the most part, to renounce their ancient way of life. Their spiritual possession of this land remains deep and absolute. In his heart every Indian knows that America belongs to him in a sense no other race can ever possess it.

Today we have to reckon, not with a dying race, but with a strong, rapidly increasing, vigorous people. In this decade Indians are said to be increasing more rapidly than any other minority group in this country. This can

[1] Indian Office figure, Jan. 1, 1943; preceding figure on Western hemisphere from National Indian Institute (includes mixed-bloods).

be explained by better health measures, a more adequate food supply, better living conditions, and perhaps most of all by the fact that a future worth living for now seems assured.

FROM RESERVATION TO MAIN STREET

James Brownhawk and many Indian youth like him still live on the Indian reservations set aside for their tribes after they were conquered by the armed force of the new country. James's people were allowed to choose land within the area of their original homes, and these acres were reserved by treaty agreement for their exclusive use.

All Indian tribes were not so fortunate. Many were forced by armed might to go to distant parts of this country where lands with definite boundary lines were reserved for them by acts of Congress in exchange for the land they had been compelled to leave. Ever since their establishment, these Indian reservations have been under the administrative control of the United States government. Originally no one except a member of the tribe was allowed to own land or to build a home within the boundaries of the reservation set aside for the tribe. Today, however, there are two types of Indian reservations in this country—the open reservation, where an Indian and a white neighbor may live side by side, because white men are now permitted to settle there; and the closed reservation that is still restricted to Indian ownership. Originally, too, no Indian could leave an

Indian reservation without permission to do so from the reservation superintendent placed in charge of the area by the United States government. This is no longer true. For more than fifty years Indians have been free to come and go across the reservation boundaries as they choose. Hundreds of Indians are today making their homes and rearing their families in the cities and towns of America just as other citizens do.

Because we hear most often about Indians who for generations have lived isolated on these reservations, we are inclined to think of the Indians in America as being outside the stream of American life. We cannot in truth think thus of a people who today are sitting beside us in the same movies, wearing the same kind of clothes, speaking the same language, or working at the same jobs. One by one, and in increasing numbers, Indian young people, and often their parents as well, are breaking through the segregation of their reservation life to become a part of the American working world.

Those of us who sat one night in the auditorium of the new building of the Department of the Interior in Washington, D. C., felt we were witnessing something in the nature of a prophecy. We had come to attend the commencement exercises of twenty-one Indian students who had accepted Civil Service appointments in the national capital. They were graduating *in absentia* from Haskell Institute, the Federal Indian school where they had received their commercial training. The pale yellow light flooding the handsome room and the music, coming softly at first, then swelling out in full ringing tones as the march began, lent an air of enchantment to the hour.

As I watched the candidates for graduation come down the aisle, I thought of all this hour stood for. Each had passed a Civil Service examination in open competition with people of every race and from every corner of the nation. Each had been appointed to a job and had been working on that job for several weeks. I knew each had done his work well for every record had been carefully checked with the employer before the student was permitted to receive the diploma of graduation. They were working in many branches of the Federal government. Two were in the Department of Justice; one in the Department of State; five had gone to the Navy Department as clerks and stenographers. They were typical of hundreds of American Indian young people all over the United States. They were also representative of young Americans of all races who had answered their country's need for skilled workers in a time of war.

And yet they were vastly different. For each carried into his new life his different racial background and the limitations and advantages this gave him. One was a Navajo who had grown up in the heart of the Arizona desert. The home of his tribe is a land of startling beauty, where strange elfin-like mesas rise abruptly from the floor of a rose and mauve desert. Two of the students came from those bleak and wind-swept plains of Montana where the Assiniboins live. Seven were Sioux from the Pine Ridge and Rosebud Indian reservations in South Dakota. Hardly more than fifty years ago their ancestors were implacable enemies of the white man. One was a Nez Percé from Idaho. His forefathers sent their messengers across half a continent of unexplored wilderness in search of the white man's Bible. One came from the Mojave Desert, which lies along the rim of the Grand Canyon. In the group were three Chippewas from Minnesota, where many Indians live as neighbors to the white residents of the state and attend public schools. Five were from Oklahoma—the state that has given so many Indian tribes sanctuary that one-third of all the Indians in the United States live within its boundaries.

There are Indians living in every state in the Union, and there are Indian reservations in almost all sections of the United States. Maine, Pennsylvania, New York, North and South Carolina, and Texas all have Indian groups living under state supervision. Most Indian reservations under Federal supervision are west of the Mississippi, but the remnant of the Seminole tribe living in Florida, the Cherokees in North Carolina, and the Choctaws in Mississippi, live on reservations under Federal control. Arizona and New Mexico rank second to Oklahoma in Indian population.

ONE PEOPLE, MANY TYPES

The group of twenty-one Haskell graduates is typical of the diverse backgrounds of Indians in the United States. Any attempt to generalize about Indians is misleading because the tribal groups vary so greatly. Any racial similarities that there may have been between many of the tribes are so far back in time as to antedate language, for many of the tribal languages are totally unrelated. The Hopi are an entirely different people from the Cherokee, yet both are Indian tribes. Their attitudes toward life are different, their racial characteristics, their language, their customs, and their traditions. And so it is with other tribes.

Some Indians are tall; others are short. Some tribes have intermarried freely with other races; other tribes have largely kept their pure Indian strain. Most tribes are very poor, living inadequately on barren and scanty land; but there are a few tribes that are comparatively rich. Some Indians are Christian; others cling to their ancient faith. Some have completely assimilated white ways; others have accepted only the superficial aspects of white culture. Some have lost their native language; others speak very little English. Some tribes have been farmers for centuries; others have not yet taken kindly to agriculture. And in between are all gradations of these differences, so that any discussion of Indians becomes almost a discussion of individuals. Lewis Meriam has pointed out that there probably is not a single statement true of all Indians, except possibly the one fact that they all possess some degree of Indian blood.[1] Even this statement can be challenged, he goes on to say, for on the

---

[1] *Facing the Future in Indian Missions*, by Lewis Meriam and George W. Hinman. New York, Friendship Press, 1932.

notes to each other via the hot rolls on the table. These
basic human emotions are alike whether one lives on an
Indian reservation or in Tallahassee or Ceylon. Environment and rearing merely alter to some degree their expression.

Indians are only one of the many minority groups that
make up our country's population. In the United States
we are all familiar with many types of environments and
varied cultures. These may have grown up out of American soil as did American Indian culture; or they may
have developed in Sweden or France or Czechoslovakia
and were transplanted and blended here. The mountain-
eer in his lonely cabin, the crowded tenement with its
broods of children, the family in the white farmhouse
in Iowa, the Texas cowboys, the Mexican sheepherders,
the Indians at their pow-wows—they are all Americans,
and American youth will be found in their midst.

So where did you meet that Indian boy you know?
Was he riding herd on a cattle range on the Pine Ridge
Indian Reservation? Or playing football at Oklahoma A.
& M. College? Was he digging potatoes on a Nebraska
farm? Herding sheep in Arizona? Fishing in that stream
in Colorado? Or working on a B-26 in Los Angeles? You
might have met him anywhere, for he is everywhere, doing all the things other young Americans are doing,
hoping for the same things other young Americans want.

At an Indian school a teacher asked her high school
class what they wanted most of all from life. The an-
swers came tumbling out: a good job; a car; a home and

tribal rolls of the Creeks and the Cherokees
ample, are the names of Negroes, ex-slaves of trib
bers, in whose veins runs not one drop of India
Indians are no more alike in interests, behavior
or intelligence than are members of any other ra
the various tribes differ as widely in languages, cu
and traditions as do the Germans, Italians, Chines
Englishmen whom you know.

There are more than two hundred different I
tribes in the United States today, speaking among
about two hundred and fifty different languages and
lects. Many of these languages are totally unrelated,
when members of different tribes wish to converse v
each other English or Spanish is used. The Pima,
pago, Pueblo, and Navajo who live in the Southw
where Spanish influence is still strong are likely to use
Spanish in talking one to the other; while those who
belong to the tribes of the plains, the Crow, the Chey
enne, the Dakota, and the Kiowa, will probably v
English.

INDIAN AMERICANS ARE NOT STRANGERS

Indian youth of today are basically like any oth
American youth. After all, the impulse that prompts o
small boy to bring home a stray puppy and another
smuggle into the *hogan* a baby prairie dog is one and t
same. And about the time Junior is asking for the c
keys to go to Youth Fellowship (and a ride afterward
the boys and girls at the Indian school are busy slippi

children; beautiful things; enough food for all the family every day; better houses—at least three or four rooms; less moving around; less sickness; movies; books; radios; peace among all people—just such a list as any young people anywhere might make.

Never before in the history of the race have there been so many young Indians leaving their reservation homes for work out in the American world as there are today. And they are proving that, given the right education and the right opportunity, Indians can achieve distinction in any field of endeavor.

A Pueblo Indian boy won first award in a national contest of original paintings sponsored for American youth by the *American Magazine*. Many young Americans of all races competed, 52,587 in all. Ten other Indian students submitted paintings. Seven of these won cash awards and one other honorable mention.

In a state-wide 4-H Club contest a Montana Indian girl won first place and was awarded a trip to the national conference in Washington, D. C.

A sixteen-year-old Indian girl graduated as the high ranking honor student from a class of one hundred and four white and Indian students.

A Chippewa Indian is commander of a destroyer in the United States Navy. He is a graduate of Annapolis and winner of the Yangtze Service Medal.

At a defense factory on the West coast Indian students are employed as rapidly as the Federal Indian school can recommend them for placement.

"The Indian boys and girls are fine workers," reports the personnel director of this plant. "Our only regret is that there are not more of them ready for employment." A Y.W.C.A. secretary gave the same report on thirty Indian girls employed at a factory she visited in the central part of the United States. "They may be somewhat slower than the other employees I have," the factory owner told her, "but they are more accurate. I would employ more Indians if I could get them."

Reports of this kind of accomplishment come from all over the country. Not all Indians succeed in making good adjustments to industrial life, of course, but there is reason to believe that as a group they are succeeding as well as are members of other groups of similar economic and educational background. No one knows the exact number of Indians employed in various types of work away from the reservations, but the estimate now exceeds forty-three thousand. In April, 1943, there were one hundred and twenty-four Indian girls enrolled as club members of one Y.W.C.A. in a western city. Seventeen of these girls were employed in defense factories, the others were in all types of jobs in every part of the city. In another large city two hundred and fifty Indians representing sixty-seven tribes were Y.W.C.A. members.

LOYALTY TO COUNTRY

Indians are giving magnificent service to their country during this period of war. All over the world where there is work to be done for America one may find Indians.

They are employed as instrument men with the United States engineers in Iceland; drivers of heavy tractors in the Canal Zone; operators of power shovels in Alaska; mechanics to repair airplanes in Australia. In this country they are working in the mines and shipyards, in the ordnance depots, in the factories, and on the railroads. And wherever they are, you will find them taking their responsibilities seriously and doing their work well. To do otherwise, they feel, would be helping the enemy.

When the United States entered World War II, Germany at once began to direct enemy propaganda at Indians, believing that since Indians in the United States were once a conquered people, they would now prove a receptive group for fifth column activities. But Germany reckoned without knowledge of the Indian heart and mind. No people in America have given more complete and unswerving loyalty to our country than have her Indian citizens. How could it be otherwise? they ask, for this is their country. Do they not belong to America more truly than any other people who live here? Have not their roots gone deeper into American soil and longest drawn nourishment there? A Canadian Indian, in a speech before the first Hemisphere Conference held at Pátzcuaro, Mexico, in 1940, put into words for all Indians their feeling for their country.

"There are many distinctions I could claim for my people," said he. "But I am satisfied with one of them—the fact that America began with us. We are the possessors of a wonderful and beautiful legacy. We are of this continent as are the mountains and the hills; the buffalo and the beavers." [1]

That is how Indians think about America. They are an inseparable part of this nation. Her destiny is their destiny, and when war once again threatened the safety of their homeland, once more they found no sacrifice too great to ask of themselves for their country's sake.

From their small population they have sent many thousands of their sons and brothers into the armed forces. Many were drafted, along with other citizens of the nation, but the percentage of voluntary enlistments is higher for Indians than for any other group in the United States except possibly the Japanese Americans. Accustomed to hardships and trained from childhood in the disciplines necessary for good soldiers, these Indian recruits are achieving brilliant records on battlefronts all over the world. They rank from private to lieutenant colonel. There are many of Indian blood who are first lieutenants, many captains, and several majors. Reports come almost daily to the Indian Office telling of the excellent morale of the Indian soldiers and of their skill and gallantry in the line of duty. Many have already been awarded medals for distinguished service.

While Indian boys are fighting and dying on foreign soil, what of their families at home? And what measure of freedom awaits those who return to their reservation homes when the war is won? In recognition of their outstanding services during World War I, all Indians born

[1] Jasper Hill, in *Indians at Work*, March, 1941.

in the United States were accorded full citizenship in 1924 by act of Congress. Now, when we are concerned for the freedom of mankind everywhere, it seems not unreasonable to hope that the people of America will accept into even greater national fellowship these once-conquered Indians who are living within the heart of the nation.

SHALL THEY KNOW FREEDOM FROM WANT?

On July 28, 1943, we heard the President of the United States say to the conquered peoples of the world:

"It is our determination to restore these conquered peoples to the dignity of human beings, masters of their own fate, entitled to freedom of speech, freedom of religion, freedom from want, freedom from fear."

Certainly these words apply equally to national policy regarding the Indian wards of the nation. Although we have, as the President stated, "started to make good on that promise" in relation to the conquered people of Europe, we have not yet put his words about "freedom from want" into effective action in the relation between this government and its dependent Indian people.

The reason must be that the facts are not known or understood. For surely the people of America would not knowingly permit Indian children and older Indian people of America, unable to provide for themselves, to live in extreme want while under the guardianship of a nation strong enough and generous enough to stretch out its arms to the ends of the world to help those of other nations who are helpless. The same morning sun that lights up the battlefields where Indian boys are fighting to establish "freedom from want" in the byways of the earth will also rise over dark and crowded hovels where Indian children in the United States exist on little more food than conquered French and Greek children have. Hunger is an old, old companion at many an Indian fireside.

"I have seen these people, the Indians," a Congressman told his colleagues on the floor of the House. "They get hungry. They grow cold. In a generation we have forced them to change from hunters to farmers, and farmers on land that the white man did not want. Only those who live among them and have seen them in their homes and know the conditions, can understand the importance of helping them."

Many Indians in the United States are living in devastating poverty. Half of the Indian families living on reservations had a family income amounting to less than $500 a year during 1943. Many families existed on an income as low as $100 a year. Over one-fourth of the total Indian population have not one square foot of land to call their own, although they are in the main a rural people depending largely on the soil for a livelihood. Four hundred years of stripping Indians of their best resources have left the overwhelming majority either landless or on arid or semi-desert land so poor that even the most skillful white farmers would be hard pressed to make a living there. Indians, unadjusted to the economic and social ways of the white world, unskilled in scientific agriculture, and without capital, barely manage to make a living. Whole Indian communities face want and destitution when, as often happens, a drought, a grasshopper scourge, or a hailstorm destroys the season's crops. Malnutrition causes lack of initiative and apathy. Lack of initiative in turn causes lack of adequate food, and so the vicious cycle is set in endless motion.

HOUSES CONDITION INDIAN WELFARE

The White House Conference on Children in Democracy has pointed out that "family life and the well-being of every member of the family are conditioned by the character of its dwelling place." Most Indian youth are compelled to grow up in overcrowded, ill-kept homes. Indian housing conditions are probably worse than those of any other group in America. An Indian child in the fourth grade has written a poem describing his home. It might be the home of countless Indian children the length and breadth of the United States.

> I have a home.
> It hasn't any floor.
> It has only one room
> And a low door.

In much of the Indian country there are no raw materials suitable for building homes. In the Great Plains area, for example, where many Indians live, there are neither stones nor brick nor lumber available and Indians are too poor to import these materials in quantities sufficient to build adequate homes. As a consequence, Indian houses are usually of inferior materials, too small, poorly ventilated, overcrowded, squalid.

Before the buffalo was destroyed, the old skin tepee was within the reach of every Indian who would hunt and tan hides if he wanted a home of his own. It was roomy, well ventilated, and clean. Civilization destroyed the source of material for this ancient home and has not yet helped the Indian to discover a low-cost building material within his economic reach to replace it. The Indian Service for the past decade has been experimenting with rammed earth as a possibility for the Great Plains area where natural building materials are scarce. But so far the experiments are not conclusive.

Many Indians do not have access to a sanitary water supply. A survey revealed that 1,004 families out of a total of 1,953 living on one reservation had to depend on water from irrigation ditches for drinking and cooking purposes. In many sections of the United States Indians have no wells but must haul their water in tubs and barrels from polluted streams. Illness and infant mortality are the inevitable results.

MISTAKEN NOTIONS OF INDIAN PROSPERITY

It is astonishing how widespread throughout this country is the erroneous belief that all Indians in the United States receive a comfortable monthly allowance from the Federal government in fulfillment of treaty obligations. This has never been true. Another false notion one meets frequently is that rations are still handed out indiscriminately as a treaty right.

When Indians were imprisoned on reservations their old means of livelihood were destroyed. Barter and hunting were no longer possible. They could not travel about for the purpose of trading. Often game was not plentiful in the barren areas assigned to them for reservations or the territory was too limited to support so many people from hunting alone. Indians did not understand the intensive agriculture practised by the European emigrant who had supplanted them. The result of all this was that the Federal government was forced to provide food for the captive Indians until they could learn some new means of providing for themselves. Often the provision of such food was included in the treaty agreements as an added inducement for the Indians to go more willingly onto the reservations. This food was distributed on a per capita basis and came to be designated as rations. Although rations were given on some reservations as a result of treaty commitments, it has been many years since this type of assistance has been handed out to Indians anywhere except on a relief basis to the sick and needy.

In 1943 the issuance of rations in any form was abolished by official order of the Commissioner of Indian Affairs and henceforward relief to Indians will be given on the same basis as that applied today in modern welfare practices among other citizens of the nation. Many Indians feel that this is a great step forward in the administration of Indian relief. "Now," said one Indian when told of the new regulation, "I shall never have to have that hated word 'rations' hurled at me again. If I am in need, I will be able to select what I want just as any other American citizen can do in the same circumstances, and I do not have to take just whatever the government wants to hand out to me."

"But," you may ask, as so many people have done who do not know the Indian situation, "does not the Federal government support the Indian people and see that they do not starve?" The Federal government does not support Indians. The great majority of the Indian population support themselves, and have done so for many, many years. The Federal government does assume responsibility for the relief of destitute Indian wards on those reservations where state relief aid is denied them. In several states Indians share fully with all other citizens in the public programs for relief of the needy; in others they share in a limited degree. But there are some states where Indians are barred from participation in the state programs of social security. For this last group the Federal government has responsibility.

How we as a nation are discharging this responsibility for the relief of needy Indians is another story. Congress has failed to appropriate sufficient funds to meet adequately the need even of the most desperate cases of Indian poverty. In 1943 the average Federal relief grant for destitute Indians amounted to only $2.52 a person a month; not because that was all the aid that was needed, but because that was all the money that was available. In the same year the states in which these needy Indians were located were providing an amount approximately three times greater for the needy of other races within the state. The Federal relief grant for Indians is not, of course, sufficient to maintain an Indian on a level compatible with the minimum standards of health and decency.

In spite of this dark picture, the future outlook for the Indian in the United States is brighter today than it has been in many decades. There is evidence on all sides that Indians on reservations are not so much set apart from the stream of American life as has been supposed. The general prosperity of the whole country in wartime is reflected on the reservations by a similar bettering of living conditions there. For example, the number of cases provided with relief by the Federal government through the Indian Service during the fiscal year 1943 declined fifty per cent as compared with a thirty-seven per cent decline in the national general relief case load for the same period. This seems to indicate that Indians are affected by the flow of events within the nation in the same manner as others. Their sons and brothers in the armed forces make their allotments for family support just as do other service men from all classes and races. And their fathers and sisters employed in industries and in agriculture throughout the nation send money to their dependents back home and so help raise the standard of living on the reservation.

CAN THERE BE FREEDOM FROM POLITICAL DISCRIMINATION?

When all Indians were made citizens of the United States in 1924 by act of Congress, it was a grudging citizenship. They were not then and are not now accorded the full privileges of democracy enjoyed by other citizens of the land. Despite their citizenship, the status of Indians in the United States is confused and complicated. Three hundred and eighty-nine treaties with the various tribes reach out of a dead past to hamper the growth and freedom of living Indians. More than four thousand laws enacted by Congress to regulate Indian affairs, piled one on the other over the passing years, multiply the confusion. Indian trust property is still being controlled by a law enacted in 1865, although both conditions and Indians have changed radically in three-quarters of a century. Congress still holds extraordinary powers over the lives and property of Indians, powers that cannot be exercised over non-Indians generally. There are states in the Union that ban Indians from attendance in the public schools, and where the unfortunate Indian—insane, blind, deaf and dumb, or feeble-minded—will not be admitted into state institutions.

Suffrage is an elementary right for any citizen of a democracy, for this is the means by which an individual can protect all other civil rights. Although they are citizens, one-fourth of the total Indian population are disfranchised by the laws of the states in which they live. Arizona denies Indians the right to vote because they are wards of the Federal government. New Mexico refuses the vote to Indians on the ground that they are "not taxed." This is done in spite of the fact that Indians in those states as elsewhere pay all forms of taxes except those on property received by them in trust from the Federal government, and in spite of the fact that whites who are not taxed do have the right to vote. A few other states discriminate against Indians as against Negroes and others by their voting requirements. Indians are refused the right to vote but are drafted into the armed forces to fill state quotas just the same as citizens who enjoy all privileges of the commonwealth.

The power that Congress holds over Indians, transcending that held over non-Indians, stems from the conception of the Federal government as guardian and protector of the Indian tribes, and of the Indian as a ward of the government. Wardship is a condition of dependence and pupilage one is born into by virtue of being an Indian, and only Congress can authorize the freeing of individual Indians from this status.

The idea of Federal guardianship of Indians grew up in the pioneer days when the Indians in this country found themselves powerless to defend themselves against aggression. Chief Justice Marshall first made the idea articulate, and, as it happened, permanent, when he ruled in 1831 in a case between the State of Georgia and the Cherokees that Indian tribes were "domestic dependent nations" and that "their relationship to the United States resembles that of a ward to a guardian."

Through the century that has passed since this historic decision, this idea of wardship has come to be applied not only to Indian tribes but to the individual members of these tribes. Not all Indians in the United States are Federal wards. Many groups of Indians are under state and not Federal supervision.

In all states except the two mentioned wardship does not affect the political freedom of Indians. In most states Indians are voters and in several communities they control the balance of voting power. In Glacier County, Montana, recently the offices of county sheriff, recorder and assessor, clerk, treasurer, and one commissioner were all held by Indians. Some of these officers have been elected repeatedly. There have been senators and representatives in Congress of Indian blood.

The reason given for the exercise of guardianship over Indians even to this day is that it is for the protection of a defenseless people. But, as Felix Cohen has written in his *Handbook of Federal Indian Law:*

The line of distinction between protection and oppression is often difficult to draw.What may seem to administrative officials and even to Congress to be a wise measure to protect the Indian against supposed infirmities of his own character, may seem to the Indian concerned a piece of presumptuous and intolerable interference with precious individual rights.[1]

Moreover, there must come a time when through education and growing strength even a once helpless people

[1] *Handbook of Federal Indian Law,* by Felix Cohen, p. 173. Washington, D. C., U. S. Printing Office.

can grow strong enough to defend themselves and no longer need someone else to do this for them. For those who reach this point, there should be some simple and uncostly means of terminating wardship.

The Home Missions Council of North America has a committee composed of representatives from the various church mission boards that is making a comprehensive study of all the implications of wardship, and the best means of working for the eventual release of Indians from this status.

WARDSHIP AND RESERVATION LIFE

To Indians such as I who work and make their permanent homes in white communities—and there are many thousands of such Indians out of the total population of 376,000—the fact of wardship might be only an occasional annoyance, or at the worst only a humiliation at being thus singled out and labeled as an incompetent person. It is the Indians who live on reservations who feel the constant pressure of wardship in all the aspects of their daily lives.

The central, dominating factor of Indian reservation life is the Federal government expressed in terms of the reservation superintendent and his staff of field employees under the Office of Indian Affairs, and the distant and extremely powerful central Indian Office. For no other citizens has the government intruded so completely into all aspects of life: property, private life, and even personal relationships. The education of all the people, adults and children alike, (with the exception of the mission schools and a few public schools on open reservations) is controlled by the Federal government. Indian trust property, which at the present writing includes livestock as well as land, is largely managed and controlled by the Federal government. Indian health, relief, housing, and agriculture are all under Federal control.

Congress delegates its power of supervision over Indians to the Secretary of the Interior, who in turn hands down these responsibilities to the Office of Indian Affairs. This government bureau, headed by a Commissioner of Indian Affairs, administers Indian property held in trust both for the tribes and for individuals; and in addition assumes authority for all the social needs of Indians on the reservations. Each reservation is in charge of a superintendent who is appointed by the Civil Service Commission upon recommendation of the Commissioner of Indian Affairs.

The superintendent of an Indian reservation has tremendous power; power that flows from real authority to manage the property of individuals and from his prestige, enhanced by the helplessness of a people unable to understand English and, therefore, inarticulate, or too poor to employ outside aid to interpret or enforce their rights. There was a time, less than a decade ago, when the reservation superintendent had complete power over the courts handling misdemeanor and other small offenses on the reservation. Often he was the jury, the prosecuting attorney, the defense lawyer, and the trial judge all in one. Much of this power was taken from him, however, and placed with the tribal courts. But even today, as long as they are on reservations, Indians are subject to Federal laws rather than state and county laws.

ALL AMERICANS ARE RESPONSIBLE

Thus, in a grimly realistic way those Indians who live on reservations are dependent upon you and me who are voters for their life, liberty, and pursuit of happiness. Congress has absolute and unreviewable power over Indian wards except that it cannot take away from them their vested rights. If you and I elect Congressmen with vision and a social conscience, the horizon of opportunity for these people widens. If, as has often happened in the past, we allow selfish interests to gain control, Indian Americans can be further plunged into an abyss of desperation and despair. The Indian Office can do no more than reflect the vision of the American people in the trends and policies it sets in motion. In the end it is you and I who determine what shall happen to these people we continue to hold in Federal wardship.

For many years friends of the Indian people watched with deepening concern the growing domination of the Federal government over the lives of the Indians and agitated for reform. In 1928, at the request of Secretary of the Interior Hubert Work, the Brookings Institution made a scientific study of the whole Indian situation

under the personal supervision of Lewis Meriam. This
magnificent appraisal of the Indians' problems marked
the real beginning of a more enlightened administration
of Indian affairs. Commissioner of Indian Affairs
Charles J. Rhoades and Assistant Commissioner Henry
J. Scattergood, who held office during President Hoover's
administration, immediately put into operation many of
the recommendations of the Meriam survey. When
John Collier succeeded to the office of Commissioner of
Indian Affairs in 1933, he also continued to carry out
still other reforms suggested by the report. Commissioner Collier, who has been a friend of long standing
to Indians and whose genius it is to understand and
value the Indian spirit, began soon after taking office
to formulate plans for a bill to submit to Congress that
would give Indians a legal right to greater self-rule.
These plans developed into the Indian Re-organization
Act, which became a law in 1934.

The Indian Re-organization Act, or the Wheeler-
Howard Act, as it was first called, was intended to free
Indians from the domination of a national government
bureau by giving them greater control over their own
affairs. The basic philosophy of this revolutionary law—
revolutionary in the thinking on Indian matters—was
simply that Indians are normal human beings, competent to manage their own affairs; that Indians possess
just as much social intelligence as any other group of
people; and that the Indian community spirit is still
alive, a dynamic, powerful current flowing strongly and

silently underneath the hard surface of government rule. A few of the main provisions of the Act are:

1. Tribes may incorporate as any municipality to exercise economic and political control over their internal affairs, and to do business; like an incorporated city they may levy taxes upon their members, regulate tribal property, administer law and order within the tribal jurisdiction.

2. The purchase of additional land for Indians is authorized; holdings originally in reservation boundaries and not yet homesteaded are restored to Indians; allotment of Indian land to individual ownership is stopped and the sale of Indian land to non-Indians curtailed.

3. A revolving loan fund provides credit to Indian tribes for agriculture and industry.

Perhaps the most revolutionary feature of this legislation was that it was not imposed on Indians without their consent. The tribes voted whether to place themselves under the law. One hundred eighty-nine tribes voted to accept the Act. Seventy-seven tribes for one reason or another preferred to continue as they were and, therefore, voted against coming under the new law. Oklahoma and Alaska were excluded by Congress from the original act, but were later placed under a similar and somewhat better law.

Some tribes have moved forward rapidly under the new law. Others have had more uneven sailing. It is only reasonable that a people so long under authoritarian control should at first find self-rule difficult. Many of the failings of Indian self-government have been exceedingly similar to those found in white communities.

This, it seems to me, is only further proof that Indians have the same faults as well as the same virtues as people of any race or culture.

"Continuing Federal guardianship," says Commissioner Collier, "can be justified if and only if the guardianship can cease to weaken the moral tissue of the Indians, can cease to be a guardianship of intellectual and moral dependency, and can become a guardianship that frees and canalizes and impels the will of the Indians and moves with them in their own movement toward positive, strong, and greatly striving independence."

This, it seems to me, expresses the intent and purpose of the Indian Re-organization Act. But the fact that such a law now exists does not solve the problem of government domination over Indians. It only gives a basis for action. There still remains a tremendous job of education both of Indians and of administration before these objectives can be achieved. The intent of any law can be frustrated by an administrator who does not believe in its principles, or by a people without the leadership to invoke its privileges.

FREEDOM OF WORSHIP—AND THE INDIAN

"Congress shall make no law respecting an establishment of religion or prohibiting the exercise thereof" was written into the Constitution of the United States by the descendants of men who came to America to find freedom of worship. Religious liberty is guaranteed to all newcomers to this land, but for many years after he was placed under the control of the Federal government the Indian could practise his ancient symbolical rites only on the sufferance of government officials. One of the first acts of the present Commissioner of Indian Affairs was to declare by official order complete religious freedom for Indians, extending to them the same constitutional right accorded to other American citizens.

FROM MANY TRIBES, ONE PEOPLE

While it is true that Indians are more and more merging into the common life of America, and that Indian youth are essentially the same as other American youth in their hopes and aspirations, Indians do have a sense of having an Indian culture that binds the whole race together in a group apart. There is an Indian heritage that unites all the different tribes, even those of most unlike traditions, by a strong feeling of racial kinship.

"Do you find that it helps in your work with the tribal councils for them to know that you are part Indian?" I asked a mixed-blood Indian employee of the Indian Service whose personal appearance happens to be more white than Indian.

"Oh, yes," he replied emphatically, "I am sure of it. I can immediately feel the tension of the group relax when I explain that I am an Indian, too, and a warm sense of friendliness comes among us like a loving presence."

I know what he meant, for I have often had the same experience. Again and again I have asked myself how to explain it. Can it be that we feel that we understand each other better because we belong to one race? Or is it more likely that we are bound together by the ties of common experiences—spiritual insights, love of beauty, and common achievements on one side, and discriminations, restrictions, and suffering on the other? Whatever the force may be that fosters this sense of oneness, it has brought together those of different families and tribes, erasing many old animosities and hatreds. Can this be prophetic? Can there be in the future about which we dream and talk a fellowship among all people, born out of the consciousness that they are children of one Father and strengthened by the experiences that come with growth and suffering?

But there were those—and they were also men
Who saw the end of sacred things and dear,
In all this wild beginning; saw with fear
Ancestral pastures gutted by the plow,
The bison, harried ceaselessly, and how
They dwindled moon by moon, with pious dread
Beheld the holy places of their dead
The mock of aliens.[1]

DO not dwell too much on the past," said a friend
in advising me on the writing of this book. "What
has passed is past, and nothing is gained by always hark-
ing back to it. What happened to the Indian in this
country is too bad, but it is over and done with. What
we want to know about now is what is happening to him
in 1944."

But deeds of such magnitude cannot be over and done
with. They do not stand alone in a period of time. Their
tentacles reach out to oncoming generations and touch
the lives of people who live centuries after the deeds
themselves are only echoes in history. I am an Indian,
living in the present *now*, but I carry the burden and the

[1] *Song of the Indian Wars*, by John G. Neihardt, p. 21. New York,
The Macmillan Co. Used by permission.

responsibility of those distant years. So do you, whether you are Indian or white. The Indian cannot be understood separated from his past, for what has happened to him over the centuries has had its large share in molding the character that is his today. That past shadows every act and thought of his life; it circumscribes his dreams; and, to a large degree, it limits his future. Thus, for the Indian, past history is living history. Only one who understands the forces compelling Indian and white relationships during those early years can comprehend the dilemma of the living Indian in our present time. As for America, it is well that she should remember those dark years lest she allow herself to be lulled once more into forgetfulness of the rights of her people.

It was over possession of his land that the struggle between the Indian and white man reached its greatest fury. At first there was friendship between the two peoples. Joyously the Indians welcomed the new immigrants to their country, thinking at first that those strange beings with white skins must be gods.

More than once the early colonists had to call on friendly Indians for help in the hard life of the frontier; more than once they were saved from starvation by men like Squanto, who in all kindliness brought them food and taught them how to fertilize the soil, how to plant and cultivate the maize he had shown them how to use. But as more and more colonists came to claim land in the new country, dark shadows began to fall across the friendship of the two races.

DEVOTION TO HOMELAND

To strike at his homeland was to strike at the very root of the Indian's racial well-being. It was not only a question of driving him to another place. In those beginning years there were vast regions unused in the sense the white man conceives land use. But to many an Indian there was only one place where he belonged—his homeland made sacred by the ageless sleep of his ancestors; made fruitful by the spirits of his children yet unborn. Here and here only for him the life-rhythm of the race could beat on in unbroken harmony.

For many tribes the earth is their mother, gentle and loving in her care for her children. Their love for the land is, therefore, a kind of mystical devotion, for this is the wise mother who has cradled the race since the beginning of time. To mutilate the fields by wastrel plowing, to denude the forests, is like laying wounds across a mother's breast. In the spring, when seeds are stirring to new life, there are tribes even today who step softly on the earth lest some rough and thoughtless movement jar her sleeping body, and, breaking the mother's rest, disturb the new seed life within her. Maize is a gift of the gods, a gift to be annually returned to the warm body of Mother Earth for tender sanctuary until the new plant is born to nourish the people.

Land belonged to all the people, to use and to cherish. That one man could buy a piece of the earth for himself, to hold against all others, was as unthinkable in

Indian philosophy as it is now to you and me that one may keep for himself a piece of the sky above us—the sky that in our European conception of the universe is the one thing man must share and use in common. In Indian economy man may keep a plot of ground for himself and his family only so long as it is used and needed.

So abhorrent to the Cherokees was the idea of parting with their fields, so terrified were they at the possibility that their homelands might be alienated, that early in their contact with the white race a tribal law was passed imposing the death penalty for any member attempting to sell any part of the tribal holdings.

Thus, for life-giving and for the sacred memories of their dead, the Indian's homeland was reverently loved. To lose that cherished relationship and to be torn from the land where their fathers slept, was to be lost indeed, for this was to be spiritually cast adrift and the life-pulse of the race to be broken.

WAR SHADOWS THE LAND

The newcomers to America could not understand this spiritual feeling that the Indians had for the land. War between the Indian who owned the land and the white man who was determined to take it was inevitable. The Indians fought to defend their very racial existence with all the skill and cunning at their command. They answered brutality with brutality, and felt that right was on their side.

"Did not God create us as well as the white people!" they cried out for understanding. "Did he not place us on the land! And give us strength and ability to defend ourselves against any invader! Does he not expect of us that we shall exert ourselves in preserving that which he gave to our forefathers, both for themselves and their offspring forever!" [1] War spread in all its fury, and all over the land the innocent of both races suffered with the guilty.

For the Indians it was a hopeless fight. Many of their wise leaders understood how hopeless.

> I saw a white Missouri flowing men
> And knew old times could never be again
> This side of where the spirit shed its load.
> Then let us give the Powder Road
> For they will take it if we do not give.
> Not all can die in battle. Some must live.[2]

The Indians had only bows and arrows with which to meet the guns and cannons of the white invaders. Suddenly warfare for them became a grim and deadly business instead of the more personal adventure and conflict that it had been in the old days before they were introduced to firearms. And in the end, they were outnumbered, for the flood of white immigrants into their country continued ever greater. The Indians were pushed back, and back, beyond one frontier after another, until

[1] *Narratives of Heckewelder*, edited by William Elsey Connelley, pp. 48-82. Cleveland, Ohio, The Burrows Brothers Co., 1910. Used by permission.

[2] *Song of the Indian Wars*, p. 34. Used by permission.

at last there was no place left where they could retreat. Driven back from their homelands onto lands claimed by other tribes, Indians saw old tribal enmities flare into new and more bitter flame, and were forced to fight each other anew and this time for space to live.

In all this struggle, Christians were not united. Some, with clear vision, saw Christ's philosophy of the Fatherhood of God in terms broad enough to include the Indian in God's family, with the right of any brother in such a family relationship. William Penn and many others like him lived firmly by this belief. When this happened there was mutual respect and friendship and justice. But other colonists, convinced that *they* were God's chosen people, clothed their destruction of Indian life with righteousness; devoutly thanked God for each Indian death; and prayed God to "send the day that puts them all to sleep." To kill an Indian, one narrator of the times wrote, would in the sight of such colonists "not only be doing God a service but also averting the wrath of God which they might otherwise incur by suffering them [the Indians] to live—they [Indians] being the same as the Canaanites of old—an accursed race who by God's command were to be destroyed." [1]

DEPORTED TO AN ALIEN LAND

Even those tribes who through all these bitter years had remained friendly to the white man were finally driven from their homes and robbed of their lands. The

[1] *Narratives of Heckewelder,* p. 153.

Cherokees, for example, were friendly. And to the last, even when forced to leave their homes, they did not resort to war. From the beginning they accepted the white man and quickly began to adopt his ways. Their daughters married the Scotch and Englishmen who came among them. Their sons were sent away to the white mission schools. Missionaries were welcomed eagerly and under their patient teaching Christianity became the faith of the tribe.

In their beautiful lands among the Alleghenies, the Cherokees were building a strong nation, neither pagan nor savage. They had a written language. So clear in concept and so perfect in organization was their alphabet, invented by one of their own leaders, that within a year of its invention there was universal literacy within the tribe. They founded a free press; there were free tribal schools; free institutions for the care of the poor and homeless. Under the direction of the missionaries they built their government and their culture into the white American pattern. They maintained law and order under their own code of laws. Their homes were comfortable, their farms well tilled, their children sturdy.

The citizens of Georgia and Tennessee envied such Indian prosperity and could not tolerate its continuance. Agitation began for removal of the Cherokees to Oklahoma. The Indians were greatly disturbed. They loved their homes. They had no interest in a wild and unknown "Indian territory." Their leaders counseled patience, urging that their treaties would protect them.

Persecutions followed agitation. No Indian had the right to so much land, so much obvious well-being, many white colonists felt. Soon the state government of Georgia listened to the clamor of its citizens and began to urge the removal of the Indians so that Cherokee lands could be annexed by the state. In December of 1829 the Georgia legislature passed an act providing that "no Indian or descendant of an Indian residing within the Creek or Cherokee Nation of Indians shall be deemed a competent witness in any court of this state to which a white man may be a party."

Denied the protection of the courts, the Cherokees living on lands claimed by Georgia were helpless to defend themselves except by war against the unscrupulous white citizens who came onto their plantations and drove them from their homes. Still the Cherokee leaders counseled peace, and still the patient people waited, believing that right and justice must prevail.

Then gold was discovered at Dahlonega, Georgia, on Indian land. A little trickle of gold. But enough to whip the cry to move the Cherokees into a frenzied crescendo. Andrew Jackson, the President of the United States, bluntly disclaimed any intention of keeping faith with the Cherokees, defied the Supreme Court ruling in favor of the Indians, and sent his troops for their removal from the state.

The Cherokee cause was lost; their confidence in the Federal government destroyed; their faith in the justice and good will of the white man grievously shaken. There was nothing for them to do except sadly to prepare for departure from the land of their forefathers.

Where were the Christian people of the nation? In the records of history their voices are strangely few. But the missionaries bring a blazing light to this dark story, for they stood solidly beside the Cherokee; counseling the bewildered people, nursing their sick and dying, going to prison in their behalf, and sharing in their exile. The church boards firmly supported their missionaries. "Do what you think is right and have no fear," the American Board counseled its workers. They carried the Cherokees' case to the Supreme Court and won for them their right to their homeland. But to no purpose.

From their loved streams and valleys, from the graves of their dead, from the life-citadel of their race, the Cherokees were deported, refugees, into an alien land. Beside them, compassionate, sharing their hardships, comforting their despair, burying their dead, the Christian missionaries journeyed into their exile. Death and misery marked that tragic journey of the tribe to the new home assigned to them in Oklahoma. The Cherokees named the route the "Trail of Tears," for thousands died on the way and lie buried along the lonely trail. Cold and hunger, fatigue, desperation, and grief snuffed out their feeble will to live. Those who lived to see Oklahoma had to devise ways to begin life all over again. They did not soon forget the sad journey, and many and vivid were the tales that they told to their children and to their children's children.

ARE INDIANS BITTER?

"Are they bitter," I have been asked, "these who have suffered so cruelly at the hands of another race?"

Some, it must be admitted, are bitter and see the white man as one who has destroyed their good life with one hand, while with the other he holds out the means of a meager existence. But the great majority are not bitter. Mature in their racial spirit, wise in their judgment of human values, they do not dwell on the wrongs of the past, knowing that good and bad exist simultaneously in all people, and that all blame cannot justly be piled on one side.

"I imagine we too did our share of dirty work in those days," chuckled a blind Apache Christian whose eyesight was destroyed by trachoma while he was held a prisoner of war by the United States government.

There are other Indians who believe that the white man has brought to their people far more than he has taken away. Cut into the foundation stone of the beautiful chapel at Bacone College, more enduring than the stone itself, is one answer that Indians have given to the world:

We have been broken up and moved six times. We have been despoiled of our property. We thought when we moved across the Missouri River and had paid for our homes in Kansas we were safe, but in a few years the white man wanted our country. We had good farms, built comfortable houses and big barns. We had schools for our children and churches where we listened to the same gospel the white man listens to. The white man came into our country from Missouri, and drove our cattle and horses away, and if our people followed them, they were killed. We try to forget these things, but we would not forget that the white man brought us the blessed gospel of Christ, the Christian's hope. This more than pays for all we have suffered.

Charles Journeycake
Chief of the Delawares

April, 1886

Blood and tears washed over these words before they could be written into stone. Charles Journeycake, chief of the Delawares, belonged to that group of Christian Indians whose tragic story is perhaps better known to the Christian world today than that of any other Indian tribe.

More than a century before the words quoted above were written a group of Delawares accepted eagerly the teaching of the Moravian missionaries who first came among them in 1735. Under Christian teaching they became a gentle people, loving peace. The converts left their tribe in order to form villages of their own where they might live "after the will and commandments of Jesus Christ." [1] Under the tutelage of the Moravian Brethren, this band of Delawares prospered, and to meet the rising hate against Indians everywhere they wore a special garb to show white men they were peaceful. This did not save them. Hatred of all Indians was so universal around the middle of the eighteenth century, and at such white heat, that even Christian Indians who

[1] *Narratives of Heckewelder.*

were minding their own business had no chance of being left in peace. The Moravian missionaries were persecuted for befriending them, and the Indians were in constant danger of annihilation.

To save themselves these Christian Indians moved westward, seeking a new land where they could worship in security and peace. Their Moravian teachers journeyed with them. The courage and temper of that group is described by one of the missionaries of their party. As they passed through the towns, he writes,

. . . the poor Indians were detained in the street. . . . A dreadful mob gathered around them, deriding, reviling, and charging them with all outrages committed by the savages, threatening to kill them on the spot; which they certainly would have done had the Indians returned evil for evil. But they were all silent, and afterwards said they comforted themselves by considering what insult and mockery our Saviour had suffered on their account.[1]

It was about 1770 when the dauntless little Christian band journeyed to Ohio, where, near the Sandusky, they established the village of Gnadenhutten. Here once again they laid out fields and planted grain, and prospered for a time. But here, as before, "their prosperity and their good fields were their undoing." Once again, as the frontier was pushed farther westward, white men

[1] *History of the Mission of the United Brethren among the Indians in North America*, by Bishop George Henry Loskiel, 1789, Pt. 2, p. 215. Translated from the German by Christian Ignatius Latrobe, 1794. Used by permission of the Board of Church Extension of the American Moravian Church.

began to say, "When we have killed the Indians the country will be ours. And the sooner this is done the better." [1]

One day a company of white men surprised some Christian Indians working in their fields. They claimed friendship and persuaded the Indians they had come to take them into their towns for protection against marauding whites. The Indians believed, and willingly returned to their village to gather their belongings. Here, defenseless, unarmed, they were brutally murdered. All were killed except two boys who escaped to warn the other villages.

Another long and weary migration began for those who were left alive. Some of her descendants say that Sally Journeycake was among the Christian Delawares who escaped. The party in which she traveled, shocked and grieved by the undeserved persecutions, is said to have renounced for a time their Christian faith. But beside the quiet campfire, after the others were lost in weary slumber, Sally Journeycake gathered the children about her to teach them Christian hymns and passages from the Bible. Charles Journeycake, chief of the Delawares, was one of these children. His people participated in forty-five treaties between the years 1778 to 1861, almost one new treaty every other year, ceding territory after territory at the demands of a stronger government. Yet he was able to declare that the gift of Christianity outweighed all the loss and tragedy that had come to

[1] Narratives of Heckewelder.

his people. Truly "the light is still shining in the darkness, for the darkness has never put it out." [1]

A BROKEN PEOPLE

I do not cite these incidents to build up sympathy for the Indian. My purpose is to show how shattered these people were, and how all-embracing was the catastrophe that had fallen on the race.

These same stories might be repeated of tribe after tribe with tragically little variation. Whether they fought back or whether they remained friendly, the tribal histories are much the same—loss of their homelands, enforced emigration, enforced idleness, poverty, segregation, defeat.

There are still living Indians who witnessed the battle at Wounded Knee in 1890, not a battle, really, but a defenseless massacre of unarmed women and children by white soldiers under military orders. On this horrible finale the Indian wars were ended; and Indians began their slow, painful struggle back to freedom. It is a struggle not yet ended.

CONFINED TO RESERVATIONS

To protect the Indian people against complete extermination and to protect the white man against the Indian, the Federal government set aside reserves of land that were to belong exclusively to the respective tribes. At first these reserves were under military con-

[1] John 1:5, Goodspeed Translation.

trol. Oklahoma was to be the great Indian territory—
far enough removed in those days to be out of the path
of white settlement. So to Oklahoma many tribes, including the Cherokees of Georgia and Tennessee, were
moved and placed on territory reserved for their exclusive use. These reservations were to be something
like a nursery where Indians could be taught white ways,
and more especially where they could be kept under
surveillance.

For more than one hundred and fifty years the Indian
had yielded ground to the advancing white man, and at
his hands had suffered grievous loss. But it was on the
reservation that the Indian was most nearly destroyed,
for here the attack on the strongholds of his spirit began. Here he lost the right to govern his own affairs,
his economic independence, and his self-reliance.

Indians did not thrive under reservation life. How
could these freedom-loving people, often transplanted
from the lands they loved, endure the ignominy of being held to a single tract of land, however wide the acre-
age? Some tribes preferred annihilation to such a life.

There came a kind of traumatism on the race from
which only today, after generations, the whole people
are beginning to emerge. Even today many tribes have
not regained their early skills in agriculture, their early
self-confidence. Something like racial shock seems to
have stopped, for a time, all impulse toward progress
for the mass of the people, holding the race imprisoned
in misery and despair. Whole generations gave them-

selves up to grief and hopelessness. Bitterness, too, had its place in the hearts of the people in those years.

"Disappointment, then a deep sadness, then a grief inexpressible," a Shoshone chief describes his people, "then at times a bitterness that makes us think of the rifle, the knife, and the tomahawk; that kindles in our hearts the fires of desperation—that, sir, is the story of our experience, of our wretched lives."

Many died of starvation and of disease induced by malnutrition. More died for want of a will to live. What was left to live for that was worth while? Those who were Christian drew heavily in those days on their faith for comfort in their agony; those who were pagan reached back to the ancients, far back to the deep wells of their racial past, for spiritual strength to endure. Reached back, and found, who knows, perhaps the same God who comforts the Christian—revealed to them in different ways. For can we believe that the Heavenly Father who loves all people with equality could deny these his children some manifestation of his love, some revelation of himself?

MEN OF GOOD WILL

It must not be thought that during all these tragic times the Indians were without friends among the white people of the nation. From the earliest history of the country there have been men of good will who have believed in the equality of rights for all mankind and who have striven to see justice and right prevail. Benjamin

Franklin, Thomas Jefferson, and many other great and very distinguished Americans lifted their voices in the Indians' behalf and championed their cause. The friends of the Indian people early organized their efforts to help them defend themselves and to work for their social advancement. The first organization of this nature was the National Indian Association, organized in the East in 1879. The Indian Rights Association, also of eastern origin, was organized in 1882 and has continued in active status to this date. It has a long and distinguished record of championship of Indian rights, of assisting in better legislation on Indian matters, and advocating progressive administration of Indian affairs. The Indian Defense Association was organized in 1924, and during its lifetime devoted itself to defending Indians against unwise legislation and in working generally for their social betterment. The Indian Defense Association later merged with the American Association on Indian Affairs, which organization is still active.

The Massachusetts Indian Association has for many years devoted itself, among other activities, to providing scholarships for advanced training to promising Indian youth. It has financed several Indian students through Dartmouth College, and has just recently financed one young Indian man through medical school at Tulane University and is now assisting another in medical school at the University of Minnesota.

The American Federation of Women's Clubs has for many years carried on an active program for Indian welfare. One of the major projects of the Indian Welfare Department of the Federation has been that of acquainting the women of the nation with the current Indian situation, and creating interest in Indian behalf. The Federation also has had as a project the financing of scholarships of nursing for Indian girls. The Daughters of the American Revolution and the National Society of the Colonial Dames of America have also provided scholarships for Indian students, and carried on other programs of work for Indians.

This does not pretend to list all the secular organizations working for the interests of the Indian people, but these will suffice to show that through the years there has been steady and persistent labor in their behalf.

"I CAME THAT THEY MAY HAVE LIFE"

Soon after the discovery of America, the Christian church began its work with the Indian people through the missionaries it sent to them; and the missionaries began their rôle, never once abandoned, as friends and defenders of the Indian's cause. Roman Catholic priests accompanied the early explorers from Spain into the Southwest, and soon after them, from another direction, came the Protestant missionaries. Some of them came to the Indian people at their own personal expense; all faced hardships and deprivations, many of them martyrdom. They were driven by a passionate desire to save souls for the Kingdom of Christ, and to bring the light of their gospel to these people who were to hear from their lips the message of Christianity for the first time.

The missionaries stayed to lead the Indians into new social and economic achievements. From the first the missionaries established schools, sometimes gathering children of Indians who were interested into their own homes for instruction. They began at once to learn the language of the people with whom they worked and to reduce it to writing so that the tribes could have the Bible in their own tongues.

"How can I provide leadership to these people if I cannot speak their language?" Father Tom, a missionary priest to Indians in Alaska, is said to have asked. "I am one, they are many. It is up to me to learn their language rather than to ask them to learn mine." This typifies the spirit of the early missionaries throughout the Indian country. After learning to speak the tribal language and reducing it to writing, the missionary then set about teaching the Indians to read and providing reading material for them. Text books, news sheets, and various portions of the Bible were translated and distributed by missionaries who found time somehow to add this difficult work to their multiple duties as ministers and teachers. For many years the Congregational Mission School at Santee, Nebraska, published a news sheet in the Dakota language and circulated it among the Dakota people.

It was the church, through its missionaries, that brought to the Indians their first schools, and built for them their first hospitals. It was the missionaries who first taught Indians how to use modern farming equipment, and who encouraged many of the tribes to practise a more settled form of agriculture. For a period of approximately three hundred years, from about 1568 to 1880, the education of all Indians was in the hands of missionary organizations. And during those years when fear and hate made of every Indian an enemy in the eyes of the white pioneer, it was the missionary who braved the scorn of his compatriots to minister to these people who were to most white men only despised and distrusted savages. In 1890, the very same year that the last and most heartless battle was fought with the Dakotas at Wounded Knee, across the continent two Christian women pitched their tent on the edge of the Navajo reservation and began there the labor of sacrificial devotion that developed into the Methodist Navajo mission at Farmington, New Mexico. While bounties were still being paid for Indian scalps by embittered white men, others of the same race were quietly facing criticism and scorn to teach Indians about the life of Christ.

To many Indians the missionaries brought the peace of freedom from doubt, and a new hope for life itself. Among these tribes the Christian teachers found a people in the deepest spiritual agony and distress, a people who believed that their ancient tribal gods had deserted them. It was not only that they had been so overwhelmingly defeated in war. Their own spiritual leadership had failed them. Again and again their holy men had promised immunity from the white man's bullets by magic wrought with the help of friendly supernatural powers. Again and again the people had seen their warriors go into battle trusting in that magic only to find death waiting among the cold shadows. It must be, the people reasoned in their hearts, that we are doomed indeed if even the spirit world has turned against us. To these lost people the missionary brought the healing message of a God who does not fail in time of trouble—a God of love, who cares for all alike, friend and foe, and who offers to Indians as well as to white men a more abundant life.

THE UNCEASING CLAMOR FOR INDIAN LAND KEPT ON

But there still remained the problem of Indian land. Our nation, eager and ruthless in its lusty youth, needed more and ever more room for expansion. There began to be pressure to reduce the size of the reservations. The Indians were a dying race, it was argued, and would, therefore, never need all the lands set aside for their use. These lands must be opened for white settlement. Congress yielded to the importunities of voters, and millions of acres of Indian lands passed from Indian ownership in this fashion.

An effort was made to devise a means of keeping at least some land for the Indian people who had failed to make progress under the reservation system. The white man began to measure Indian needs—as the white man ever has done and continues to do—by his own standards. The highest desire of the European peasant is to own his own tract of land. The driving force behind Anglo-Saxon achievement is the accumulation of personal property. Not remembering, indeed not even knowing in many instances, the Indian's attitude toward his land, his friends—his sincere friends—who wanted only to help him, began to argue that if he could but own his little tract of land for his exclusive self, his whole attitude toward life would be revolutionized.

This blind belief that one man's motivation must be another's ignored the Indians' whole cultural outlook on land and on life. Secure in their belief that this would be the stimulant needed to arouse a stunned and broken people to new life, Congress passed the Allotment Act in 1887 providing for the partitioning of Indian lands into individual ownership.

There is much documentary evidence that most full-blood Indians and all other Indians who still lived by the Indian way of life did not want their lands allotted. Delegations came to Washington to plead with Congress against it; met congressional committees in their towns. They pled in vain for the enforcement of their old treaties guaranteeing their lands to the tribe. They foretold what finally came to pass, that the lands would be lost to the people. Apparently no one at the time considered that the Indian might know best what was for his own good and the good of his people. The white man wanted allotment, believed in allotment, and many mixed-bloods, traveling in white ways, wanted the land divided so that they might have their share. So the Act was passed.

HOW THE ALLOTMENT ACT WORKED

The colossal failure of the allotment scheme, so far as its educational purpose is concerned, is now a matter of history. In forty-seven short years after the passage of the Act Indian land holdings dwindled from an estimated 138,000,000 acres to fewer than 52,000,000 acres.[1] Usually it was the best land that passed out of Indian ownership, the blackest soil, the richest forests. Sometimes this was through exploitation; sometimes through plain buying and selling. But of 52,000,000 acres that today remain in Indian possession much is desert or semi-desert. On it must somehow be found a way to support a rapidly growing population. For contrary to all expectations, the Indian is not a dying race but a rapidly increasing, strongly rural people for whom some future hope must be found.

The problems attendant upon the partition of Indian lands into individual holdings have proved to be multitudinous.

For example, Jim Runningwolf is typical of much of the Indian population. He doesn't know how to farm. His people were hunters. But he sits on his allotment wishing someone would come along and show him what to do. The Indian Agent comes along.

[1] National Resources Report, Part X.

"You are not using your land," he says to Jim. "Why don't you let me lease it for you to that white farmer who was looking it over the other day?" All right with Jim. The government has always insisted it knew best anyway. So Jim Runningwolf and many others like him become petty landlords living in idleness on an annual rent barely sufficient to hold off starvation—never enough to lift the shadow of malnutrition from their households.

Then there is the problem of heirship. When Jim Runningwolf dies there will be four daughters and one son to inherit his one hundred and sixty acres. No one of the five heirs has enough money to buy out the other four. The usual way a white family handles such a situation is for the family member who wants to keep the farm to mortgage the land for enough to buy out the other heirs. The Runningwolf heirs can't do this for this land cannot be sold because Jim Runningwolf is a ward. So, in the absence of a will, the only thing to do would be to partition his land among the five heirs. In a country ill adapted to agriculture, thirty-five acres are not worth much money, so the land will probably not be partitioned. Instead, the government will go on leasing the land, dividing the lease money among the heirs down through the generations.

There are pieces of land on the books of the Indian Office so divided among heirs that the annual lease income therefrom to any one heir is less than one cent. Yet the annual cost to the government to administer the estate is estimated at approximately fifty times as much as the annual lease the heir receives.

By 1934 when the passage of the Indian Re-organization Act stopped the flow of Indian lands from Indian ownership, already there were more than one hundred thousand landless Indians, and at least another hundred thousand whose lands cannot adequately support the people depending on it for a living. Such lands—as the Navajo, for example—are already over-grazed and dangerously eroded. While some lands have been purchased to re-establish the landless Indians, available funds are woefully inadequate to the need. For many Indian youth who wish to remain on the reservations, there is no land. Yet these are a rural people who bring to the soil a spiritual passion that could enrich American life. Our naked hillsides, our emptied streams, our starved and barren soil, depleted by two centuries of careless farming, cry out the extremity of America's need for their gift. How can the Indians be helped to make their racial feeling for the soil more potent in their own practical lives, and in the life of the nation?

UNSOLVED PROBLEMS OF LAND USE

Two great problems relating to Indian land use are yet unsolved: how to secure an adequate land base for approximately two-thirds of the Indian population, and how to teach the Indian to make maximum use of the resources he now has. It is true that Indians do not yet understand land use as the white man knows the purposes for land, and that consequently much of the Indian land is now being leased by white farmers. If this could be returned to intensive use by the Indians themselves, there would be greater economic stability for all members of the tribe.

Progress is being made in this direction: soil is being built up by better cultivation and grazing practices; and improved quality of stock is increasing Indian income. The Indians themselves are beginning to tackle some of their complicated land problems. There is evidence of new incentive and new vitality in a people whose outlook on life was formerly one of hopelessness.

So far the church is only beginning to meet the challenge of the Indian communities at this point. We have too often failed to see that a body made listless by undernourishment can seldom house a vigorous spirit. We have not well enough understood that if the church is to bring a more abundant life to these people it must have active concern for their social and economic ills. The Indians are a rural people, deeply attached to the soil, but for many of them agriculture is still insecurely grafted onto their cultural structure; and all of them need to understand and use better agricultural methods, more scientific practices, if they are to survive. Leadership is needed at every step. Too often the church has been content to leave that leadership to the Federal government, feeling no responsibility for whatever motivation, whatever inspiration may be needed to spur the community to greater economic achievement.

I know one church in the Indian country whose minister is inspiring his parishioners to use their land instead of leasing it; who is saying constantly in his sermons that farming is a good life, and proving his beliefs by practising them. This pastor keeps in his study all the latest information on how to poison grasshoppers; how to stop soil erosion; how to raise poultry; how to produce better crops—all the things he can find that his parishioners need to know in order to become better farmers. He is working out with the men of his church various ways to pool their limited resources so each man can profit from the efforts of many. His men come to him in difficulties of farming as well as difficulties of the spirit. He has stimulated organization of a 4-H Club among the young people of his parish and on occasions he has gone with his members to attend short courses at the state agricultural college. There is need for many more ministers of this type to work with people of all races.

While change, deep and profound, beats remorselessly against the citadel of the race, Indian life flows on. Generations live and die and new generations are born. Out of the framework of this past Indian youth must advance to face the world. Where do they find their strength? On what can they build their faith? For strength they have without question and faith they have without measure—faith in their right to a part in the building of this, their country.

"It is our task," declares a bishop of a great church,

"our bounden duty, to help them along the trail which we have forced them to travel for our own profit, and to make it possible for them to take an honored place in our common life to which they have so many splendid qualities to contribute."

STRONG IS THE INDIAN SPIRIT

> With beauty before me, may I walk.
> With beauty behind me, may I walk.
> With beauty below me, may I walk.
> With beauty all around me, may I walk.
> —Navajo

ON a trail of fading beauty, twilight moved across
the valley. The lights from the distant city twin-
kled through the gathering dusk like happy fireflies,
deepening the feeling of comradeship already strong
among the group of Indian students gathered on the
broad porch of the campus recreation hall. It was not a
meeting someone had called. As so frequently happened
on this campus, a group of students from many tribes
had drifted together just for talk. Tonight the talk had
played lightly on many things. Then it chanced upon
the Indian ways of life, the ancient Indian beliefs.

"What do they mean," someone asked, "when they
say we should hold fast to that which is Indian in our
lives?" Then questions came fast and eagerly.

"In a world dominated by aggressive competition is
there room for those racial ideals and purposes, those
incentives and ways of looking at life that make up

Indian culture, and distinguish an Indian from other people?"

"Can one be Christian and still follow the Indian way?"

"Has the Indian anything to give to the white man?"

As these young people talked together on this evening and many others, they discovered leads to help them answer these difficult questions for themselves.

WHAT CULTURAL DIFFERENCES MEAN

Doctors Alexander and Dorothea Leighton, who have just recently made a study of the Navajo religion, have given an excellent illustration of the meaning of cultural differences between people, and the significance of cultural values. After describing a Navajo ceremonial for a sick Navajo patient, they say:

The patient stands facing the West, breathing in the dawn four times. A white man who stood beside him would see the yellow day coming up over miles and miles of sage, a copse of piñons, three or four old yellow pines in the soft volcanic cone, and very far away the snowy top of Mount Taylor.

Compare what the Navajo could see looking at the same landscape. The sage-covered earth is Changing Woman, one of the most benevolent of the gods, who grows old and young again with the cycle of each year's seasons. The rising sun is himself a god who with Changing Woman produced a warrior that rid the earth of most of its evil forces and who is still using his powers to help people. The first brightness is another god, Dawn-Boy, and to the north, south, east, and west the Navajo can see toward the homes of other deities. To the north is bitter, unhappy First Woman, who sends colds and sickness; to the south is the Gila Monster, who helps diagnosticians reveal the unknown. The cone-shaped mountains have lava on their sides, which is the caked blood of a wicked giant killed by the Sun's warrior offspring, and lies as modern evidence of the truth of Navajo tradition. The white peak of Mount Taylor is the top of Turquoise Mountain, built and decorated by the Hogan God, who later knocked its top off in a rage when he could not get the name for it he wanted, and forbade any living thing to try to reach the top.

After citing this contrast between Indian and white views of the same scene, the Drs. Leighton go on to say:

It is true that all human beings have the same "dimensions, senses, affections, and passions," but these affections and passions are not all roused by the same things, and there lie the seeds of misunderstanding and conflict imbedded in culture.[1]

While the white race has been forging out a technological civilization, the Indian on this continent was building a way of life that, from the very core, concerned itself with the relationship of man to man, and of man to the spirit. It is not a perfect structure, for the Indian, like the rest of mankind, is very human and subject to all human weakness. But it had beauty, and steadfastness of purpose. The Indian way of life is still alive in many parts of this country, a pulsating, vital force in

[1] "Elements of Psychotherapy in Navajo Religion," by Alexander H. and Dorothea C. Leighton, in *Psychiatry*, 4, 1941, pp. 515-523.

the lives of the people. Indian youth are still conditioned by the ancient Indian patterns.

Some of these ways cannot fit into a modern world, and so will have to be discarded. There are shadows in Indian life, as in the lives of all people. Superstition and fear, for example, still burden many Indians. The rule of the old men, still found today in much of the Indian country, often stifles the adventurous spirit of youth, and stands in the way of progress. The weight of tradition sometimes pulls like a heavy chain against advancement. Even the practice of family sharing, good in itself and necessary for its time, frequently proves a handicap to Indian youth who wish to accept white civilization, which puts its emphasis on individual achievement. These are only a few of the shadows in the Indian way of life. But there are also surviving values that are good and that the Indians believe we would do well to retain in American life. All people would be richer for sharing them.

In the strictest sense, there is actually no one Indian way of life, for each Indian tribe has its own customs, its own religious beliefs, and its own ways of looking at life. But through the ways of all the tribes of the United States, there runs a golden thread of similarity of thought that makes it possible for us to say with some measure of truth, "This is the Indian way of doing things." Even to speak thus generally does not imply that every individual Indian thinks or acts in such a manner, any more than to say, "Christians love one another," truly means that all Christians have achieved that love. We can only mean that this is the ideal that Christians generally strive to attain. Therefore, in the following discussion of the positive values in Indian life that we who are Indian would do well to hold onto, I have endeavored to list only those elements found to be more or less general among all the tribes, with conscious appreciation that all Indians do not achieve the highest ideals of their beliefs any more than do people of other faiths and practices.

REVERENCE AND HUMILITY ARE VALUES TO BE RETAINED

The Indian is profoundly religious and deeply reverent. The names of his gods are often too sacred to be said aloud, and it is to him unthinkable to speak of them lightly or profanely. The poor man in Indian society, the man to be pitied, is the man without spiritual vision. Through all the life of the race, religion has been as essential to well-being as food and water, for spiritual forces permeate the whole of life on the face of the earth and sustain the life of the people. The trees and the seeds, the animals, the wind, all earthly life share with man the mysterious source of life in the heavens, and like man draw upon it for spiritual power. Even the days of the week, the Maya believed, were once gods and so not to be considered lightly.

Survival for the Indian has always meant a desperate struggle against the elements of nature, against despoiling enemies, against cold and hunger. Without science to help him, with only his two hands and the strength his gods might yield him, the Indian has learned to know with the clearness of reality the pitiful limitations of mankind. With spiritual insight born of humility, he turns to divine power for help. Prayer is as natural for him as the passing of night and day, for all the acts of his life are marked with deep religious significance. The rituals, the ceremonials, the sacred songs are a form of prayer—a yearning search for unity with the Mysterious Power at the heart of the universe whom the Christians know as God.

In times of great stress or intense longing, passive prayer is not enough. Then by his music, his dancing, his sacred races, the Indian identifies his effort with the efforts of the spiritual power, thereby seeking to increase the strength of both. "Work with us, work with us" is the burden of his ritual songs. Forty men dancing and singing in unison on the Plaza of Zuñi help the gods to bring rain. Indian young men race to add their physical strength to the spiritual energy of their gods, to help bring rain, to help the Sun on his endless journey across the heavens.

> Swift is our racing, for
> We bring our strength, O Sun Father,
> To aid you in your tireless race;
> So may our people endure.
> —Pueblo [1]

[1] "Indian Choral Songs," by Nellie Barnes, in *The Southwest Review*, Vol. XIII, July, 1928, p. 481. Used by permission.

Thus, the eternal search of man for God goes on in Indian life, as among all people, flowering in deep spiritual insight and beauty.

The complete integration of their religion with the whole of life makes it difficult for many Indians to understand some of the practices of Christianity they see about them, for often it seems to them that it is possible for the Christian to separate his religious and secular life. Recently an educated Hopi who had tried being a Christian returned to his village and to the faith of the ancient Hopi. When asked why, he replied that he had not found his experience in the Christian world satisfying. The white man seemed to him to remember his religion only a few hours each day and to relegate his serious worship to one day each week, whereas, with the Hopi, religion is needed and expressed in every act of his life, even in his dreams, for wisdom is often revealed to him in dreams. "Strange that the white man is no better after having had it so long," a pagan Cherokee is said to have remarked in wonder upon being read passages from the *Gospel of St. Mark*.[1]

But there are many other Indians who understand that among white men, as among men of their own race, there are those who are not spiritually wise enough to understand the highest ideals of the religion in which they believe, and others who, though they understand, are not strong enough to live up to its teachings. These

[1] *Cherokee Messenger*, by Althea Bass. Norman, Oklahoma, University of Oklahoma Press, 1936.

Indians do not measure the strength of Christianity by the shortcomings of its followers. And many, many Indians from this number have cut loose from their old Indian faiths and have stood firm in Christianity through all the difficulties and discouragements of a lifetime, finding in the Christian way of life more deep and abiding satisfactions than any they had ever known.

THE INDIAN'S RELATIONSHIP TO THE NATURAL WORLD

The Indian was not a child of nature, as many writers have pictured him. He was an adult in balance with the universe about him. He did not seek to control nature; rather he placed himself in harmony with her laws and yielded himself to her care as did the animals and the trees who were his brothers. He believed in the relationship of all life, and that all of life was bound together by mutual need and mutual origin.

So the Indian used from the natural world about him only what was necessary to sustain life. If trees had to be cut for shelter, a prayer was said to atone for the act and to release the life-power within it. If an animal must be killed for food or clothing, the God of life was appeased by the need of the people. Among some tribes organized methods of conservation were practised throughout the Indian world long before the white man came to America. Each family had its own traditional hunting grounds and these were kept stocked with game by careful rotation in hunting. To destroy for the wanton pleasure of killing was sacrilegious and incomprehensible. After more than twenty thousand years of use the Indian turned over to the white man woods and streams and mountains in all their pristine loveliness and plenty.

Science is at last showing us that this ancient Indian concept of the organic wholeness of all life was not merely the blind meaningless dream of an untutored savage. We now know, for example, that even the contribution of the lowly earthworm is essential to the well-being of mankind. Without its efforts in pulverizing the soil, no plant life can flourish. Where it has been destroyed the soil is poorer, plant life suffers, and poverty among men increases. It has taken us a long time to learn, but we have finally understood that when bird life is gone, destructive forces multiply unchecked to the detriment of man. So we are slowly beginning to comprehend how all forms of life are dependent one upon the other.

Thus the Indian, through centuries of trial and error, learned to live with the natural world. Nature is still his teacher, filling every crevice of his life, every fragment of his imagination. In his music is the beat of the eagle's wing, the rhythm of the leaves, the soft rush of the evening wind. His poetry is full of its imagery.

> Swift and far I journey,
> Swift upon the rainbow.[1]

[1] *The Indians' Book*, edited by Natalie Curtis Burlin, p. 354. New York, Harper & Brothers, 1937. Used by permission.

> We are the stars which sing,
> We sing with our light;
> We are the birds of fire,
> We fly over the sky.
> Our light is a voice;
> We make a road for the spirits,
> For the spirits to pass over.[1]

When chaos and disaster threaten to engulf the Indian in despair, he renews the strength of his spirit in communion with his earth brothers, the deer, the fox, the wren, the creeping snail. He sees their life go on in ceaseless ritual, life, death, and life again, in one beautiful pulsing chord. And here he finds deep courage, for he knows that he too is one of these, and that for him also, and for his people, as for the trees, the rain, the animal brothers, life shall beat on, beautiful, harmonious, everlasting.

IT IS MORE BLESSED TO GIVE THAN TO RECEIVE

There are Indian communities today where it is truly more blessed to give than to receive. Generosity here is not an ideal to be aimed at; it is a way of life, taught from the cradle and practised joyously into old age. Here man achieves prestige, not by the wealth he accumulates for himself, but by the wealth he gives away! Among the Dakotas, giving is the great rule of life. At the death of a loved one, at a feast of honor, or any ceremonial occa-

[1] *Algonquin Legends of New England*, by Charles G. Leland, p. 379. Boston, Houghton Mifflin Co. Used by permission.

STRONG IS THE INDIAN SPIRIT

sion, whatever one prized most highly was given away as a token of esteem and honor. By this means, these people maintained their ancient democracy. Within the tribe there were no very rich, no very poor, for all the people shared the provisions furnished by the strong and skillful. There was no upper class, no middle class, no lower class. All men were equal and all men shared. Even today in Indian communities it is no stigma to be poor in material possessions. The deep, the biting disgrace, comes from being stingy, from hoarding for oneself that which another needs, from withholding from another what one can give.

Children are still carefully trained to find deep satisfaction in giving, for in this manner the Indian expresses his loyalty to his group and receives their loyalty in return. Sharing with the weak, the helpless, and the poor within the tribe is universal in Indian culture. In all Indian groups this is the expected, normal social behavior. In the Pueblo villages of the Southwest, for example, the strong members of the village accept as a matter of course responsibility for harvesting the fields and tending the flocks of the widows and aged, or the sick and helpless.

Since Indians are human, there have always been men of greed and selfishness among them as among all people. Indian legends tell of them, and in these tales the stingy man always comes to some unhappy fate. So also are there legends of good men who act as good men ought to act in the Indian way of life.

My friends, [the legend tells us of one of these] this man has done as a Hunka should do. He has given all that he had. He took the food from his mouth and divided with me. He gave me his moccasins, his shirt, and his leggings, and now he is naked and has nothing.

I will put this red stripe on his face so the people may see it and know that he has given all his possessions away . . . so that they will remember this day, and when they see one in want they will give to that one.[1]

In another age, on a distant hillside of a far-off country, the Son of Man related to his followers a similar story:

For I was hungry, and ye gave me to eat; I was thirsty, and ye gave me drink; I was a stranger, and ye took me in; naked, and ye clothed me; I was sick, and ye visited me; I was in prison, and ye came unto me.[2]

Hospitality is but another form of generosity. Indian hospitality has been known and written about since the first white man came to the shores of America. Columbus and his sailors were welcomed joyously into the homes of the people. An enemy who came in peace, or a friend, was accepted as a member of the household. Even today, when food has become a constant anxiety, any guest is welcome to share in a truly Indian household until the larder is empty, and it is base to begrudge the food that is eaten. It is the Indian way to give, and to give freely.

[1] *Anthropological Papers of the American Museum of Natural History*, Vol. 16, p. 139. Used by permission.
[2] Matthew 25:35-36.

It is perhaps at this point that the Indian has found the white way of life most difficult to understand.

If a white man in traveling through our country [Benjamin Franklin reports an Indian as saying] enters one of our cabins, we all treat him as I treat you. We dry him if he is wet, we warm him if he is cold, and give him meat and drink that he may allay his thirst and hunger; we spread soft furs for him to rest and sleep on. We demand nothing in return. But if I go into a white man's house in Albany and ask for victuals and drink, they say, "Where is your money?" and if I have none, they say, "Get out." . . . You see they have not learned those little good things we need no meeting to be instructed in because our mothers taught them to us when we were children.[1]

SERVICE TO COMMUNITY AN IDEAL OF INDIAN LIFE

Indian life, when left to shape itself according to the Indian pattern, is built on the principles of democracy. Mutual interest, mutual sharing, and equality, all within the tribe, are the dominant characteristics. In the old days, Indian communities were kept small, rarely numbering more than one to two hundred persons. If the circle began to grow too large for effective cooperative effort, some leader broke away and formed another band. Each band had complete freedom of action but the eternal preoccupation of all members was group welfare rather than individual advantage. The prayer of the In-

[1] "Remarks Concerning the Savages of North America," by Benjamin Franklin.

dian mother was that her infant might grow up and be useful to the tribe.

"Guard your tongue in your youth," Old Chief Wabashaw advised, "and in age you may mature a thought that will be of service to your people." An Indian youth was never allowed to forget that his first duty was not to himself but to the tribe and clan. Prestige came from service to the community. The controlling emphasis of all education was upon maintaining good group relationships. The individual must not act in such a way that life in the group was made unpleasant. There are tribes who believe that one must not grieve too openly lest those all about one be made unhappy. One must not be upset, full of anger, for this disturbs the equanimity of others. If life is to be harmonious in such intimate relationships, there must be the most careful, thoughtful consideration of other group members. This was the ideal and this accounts in part for the unfailing courtesy and dignity encountered among all Indian tribes.

This feeling of group responsibility and interest is still one of the strongest elements in Indian life. Songs and dances are still mediums to bind the people together in unity of purpose. Indian communities still work together, play together, and share equally in common responsibilities and perils. Indians are going away from the reservations in groups to find work, and they live together as one group when they reach employment centers. They are joining together in cooperative efforts for economic rehabilitation. Only recently the Jicarilla

Apaches refused to lease their individual lands for oil except on the basis that all the tribe share equally in whatever mineral resources might be developed.

In all this group organization, the individual is important. Few decisions are made that are not unanimous decisions. The Papagos, for example, believe that a problem can be talked out and discussions go on until unanimity is reached. Every individual has an active share in making plans and definite responsibilities for group welfare. This gives his life significance and validity. Within the framework of the group life, there is freedom for individual differences and reverence for personality. Even the personality of the child is respected, for Indian parents do not dominate their children.

INDIAN CHILDREN ARE THE STRENGTH OF THE TRIBE

Indian childhood is a happy experience. There is no grown-up world from which children are excluded. Play and responsibility blend happily together under Indian teaching so that it is difficult to sense where one leaves off and the other begins. Children share in many adult activities. They dance in the ceremonials, dressed as their parents dress, moving their tiny feet in the dance as best they are able. They accompany the adults to church. They copy the tasks of the household and are calmly expected to carry as much responsibility as their skills and age will allow them. No one is too hurried to answer their questions, to make them feel they are members of the community with rights and personalities to be respected. Grandmothers cradle them, teach them the disciplines necessary to live as an Indian and the accepted social behavior. The old men tell them the ancient tales, sing them the ancient songs, over and over and over again until the great purposes of the race, the history, the tribal lore, are as truly theirs as their racial blood stream.

DISCIPLINES FOR LIVING

Courage, endurance, patience, and a steadfast personal dignity are the age-old disciplines taught to Indian youth from the cradle. Indian life has always been full of hardship, and strength to endure was necessary for survival. Indians had to be schooled to withstand long stretches of hunger, sudden times of plenty, cold, hours of unremitting toil, ruinous warfare, endless treks over difficult trails, and to face all with equanimity.

Sacajawea could never have led Lewis and Clark to claim the great West for America had she not been rigorously trained in these ancient disciplines. Constant, patient observations along the trail and in the heavens were essential to help her find the way through that uncharted wilderness. A sure knowledge of the stars and the ways of the sun was necessary to determine direction; acquaintance with the signs of the trail, to avoid danger; familiarity with the fruits and berries, to supply food for the weary travelers. Strength to endure the endless march, courage, and a cool head were the gifts from her way of life that enabled this simple Indian woman to render her nation so great a service. When the boats capsized on the journey it was Sacajawea who, at the risk of her life, rescued the boats and precious instruments so vital to success of the venture.

Courage is linked with pride of race in Indian thinking. Courage to keep the race living, to endure for the future generations, has been the eternal preoccupation of the tribal fathers from ancient times down to today. "Be proud that the Great Spirit designed you to be an Indian," a chieftain is said to have told his son. "Let no man say an Indian asked for mercy," another scornfully told his captors. It is a reflection on the strength of the whole people to show fear to an enemy, to be unable to endure torture.

"Is not the fire of the invaders just a little hot?" asked his companion of Cuauhtemoc while the Spaniards were burning the feet of these two Indian captives to force them to tell the secret of a buried treasure. Cuauhtemoc smiled his reply. "Think you I am resting on a bed of roses?" He was lamed for life, but the secret remained his and the Spaniards saw no expression of pain.[1]

Patience is a discipline of the Indians. Their ability to wait endlessly in calm resignation, their remarkable survival in the face of devastating wars and exploitation, testify to an endless patience. An Indian of the Pine Ridge Reservation claims that for twenty years his com-

[1] "The Story of Education in Mexico," by Herberto M. Sein, in *Indians at Work*, February, 1941.

munity has planted gardens only to have them destroyed by drought or grasshoppers. Yet in the face of repeated failure, somewhere, somehow, this Indian community has found the patience and faith to plant again at each new growing season.

GIFTS INDIANS HAVE MADE TO THE WORLD

It is these disciplines that have enabled Indians to make rich gifts to society. Much of the food of the world comes from their painstaking efforts. Corn is not the hardy, staple food it is today by accident. It was developed from a tiny tropical plant to the product we know today through long years of patient cultivation by Indian farmers. Beans, pumpkin, chocolate, peanuts, and squash are a few of many foods Indians have contributed to the world's food supply. Ireland owes her survival in part to Indians, for it was the white and sweet potatoes developed by Indians that helped to rescue her people from famine.

Indian sports of canoeing, tobogganing, snowshoeing, lacrosse, and other forms of ball games have increased the enjoyment of all nations. The Indian's methods of hunting and fishing, his forms of archery and techniques of woodcraft, have added to the world's pleasure. At least half the names of the states of our country are Indian, while hundreds of cities and towns, lakes and rivers, will forever carry in their names the poetry and beauty of the Indian's language. It was the Indian who first discovered and used the strategic locations that are now the sites of America's principal cities. His trade routes and trails have become the routes of our modern highways and railroads. His beautiful arts and crafts are increasingly adding to the joy and pleasure of all people.

The flower and fruit of the Indian way of life, the expression of its power and beauty, are found in the native arts, in the exquisite painting, the music, the songs, the artistic crafts, the colorful pageantry and rituals. Indian art related itself completely to Indian life. Ceremonials grew out of the people's daily needs and experiences, and all their art forms blossomed out of a life that was to them joyous and beautiful. All the people shared in the making of songs, in the rhythm of the dances, in the making of beautiful articles for daily use. Indians believed that even the songs held spiritual power, and the women eased the backbreaking labor of preparing the bread by the rhythm of corn-grinding songs filled with beautiful imagery.

Each product made by the Indian artist had some specific functional purpose. Everyday articles for common use, such as baskets for storing grain, pottery for holding water, utensils for cooking, were lovingly decorated. So completely universal was the art life of the people, so all-pervading in Indian life was the striving for skillful workmanship and beauty, that even today the majority of Indians have a strong sense of rhythm, and a lavish gift for color and imaginative design. They are artists whose spirits respond to beauty in all of its forms.

GIFTS OF THE SPIRIT

While the Indian has made numerous material contributions to white culture, may not his greatest gifts prove to be spiritual ones—his unyielding will to live; his faith in his own destiny; his charity, his courage and steadfastness; his ideal of equality; and his love of beauty? These things out of Indian life are good and fit for use in any desirable world—the spiritual insight that grows with reverence and worship; the harmonious love and understanding of the earth and all nature; generosity, hospitality, the love of little children; responsibility to one's group, cooperation; the integrity of the individual; endurance, courage, patience, and a sense of unity with one's past. These are some of the positive forces still vibrantly alive in many Indian communities today— some of the values that still have meaning for many of the Indian young people who will carry them into tomorrow.

DARE WE LET INDIANS DO THEIR OWN THINKING?

What to prune and what to retain of the Indian way of life must in the end be decided by Indians themselves. Like unwise parents, the Federal government and the church, both concerned with the schooling of Indian youth, have in the past often denied to Indians their right of self-determination by deciding many issues for them. This has been done frequently without under-

standing Indian purposes and tendencies and all un-
mindful of the full consequences that the destruction
of one element in Indian life may have on the total
interrelated structure.

There are many illustrations to be cited to show how
white concepts of life have been forced on the Indian
people. The most familiar one, that of the white concept of land tenure, has already been discussed at length.
There are other examples in almost every realm of Indian thought. In the early days, even as late as 1925,
Indian children in the schools were forbidden to speak
the tribal language, the quicker to inculcate them with
the complete principles of the white ways of life. When
the language of a people is destroyed, much of the life
out of which it came is destroyed with it.

Indian parents, for many years, had no choice of
whether or not their children should be sent away to be
educated out of the reach of parental care and instruction, for this decision lay entirely in the hands of the
Federal government. Nor could Indians decide of their
own volition when and what religious ceremonials they
might hold, for this, too, was decided for them by government officials. In the early days some zealous missionaries, confusing white culture with Christianity, insisted
that the new Indian convert to the Christian faith must
cut off his long braids or his Indian scalp lock, and don
the garb of the white man before, in the opinion of the
missionary, he could be acceptable in the Lord's sight.
Happily those days are now past. Children are no longer

taken from their homes without parental consent, and in the schools children may speak the tribal languages as they choose. Around the altars of the church, men in long braids and men wearing blankets or buckskin moccasins are just as acceptable as the men who come to the service in blue serge suits.

A new spirit of understanding and of appreciation of the right of people to their differences is abroad in the world, and a new willingness to recognize worth and value in those differences. This new policy of allowing people to determine for themselves those fundamental issues affecting their lives is beginning to operate for Indians as for other minority groups of the world.

But the battle is not yet won. There are many questions to be answered. Should the Navajo medicine man be given the same recognition as any other religious or medical practitioner? Are Indian religious ceremonials to be allowed or forcibly curtailed? What does freedom of worship imply for the Indian? Should Indians have more to say about the educational policies of the Federal government that determine the future of their children? These questions suggest just a few of the problems still to be solved.

The function of those organizations that would help Indian youth in the future must be to help them to discover their own capacities, to discriminate, and to blend into a workable relationship with the more dominant world those elements of Indian culture that can be of benefit to Indians and to the world. It must not be to make parental decisions or to enforce what officials might look upon as progress.

CHANGE IS AN OLD STORY TO INDIANS

Indian culture is not now, and never has been, static. Indians have all through the ages demonstrated a capacity to change and to assimilate and still remain Indian. The urge for the new and adventurous that drove their ancestors from out of the heart of Asia in search of a new world has manifested itself again and again in the willingness of the people to appropriate new ideas and to make them their own. The Navajo took weaving from the Pueblo, silver from the Mexican, wool from the Spanish. Yet these things the Navajo has made completely, irrevocably his own, tools for the expression of concepts intrinsically Navajo. Thus the Indian clings to the familiar while he seeks new ways.

The horse has been in the romantic idea of many white men as much an integral part of the warlike Plains Indian as his eagle feathers and his colorful history, yet the horse was not used by Indians before the Spaniards came. The Plains tribes accepted this new mode of travel so completely that their whole manner of living was changed. Their food habits, their type of abode, their vocations and political institutions, even their religious concepts, now began to center about a hunting life. They gave up their little plots of farm land beside the streams to follow the hunt, their earth houses for the more easily movable skin tepee, their sedentary life for one of mobility. Yet fundamentally, basically, spiritually, the Plains tribes remained Indian.

Indian traders, moving among the tribes long before the white man came to America, carried new ideas and new ways across the length of the Western Hemisphere, from east to west, from north to south, from group to group among Indians, as traders have done throughout all the history of mankind. Handspun cotton mantas from the Pueblo, fiber weaving from the Navajo, corn from Mexico, turquoise from the Southwest, pearls from Ohio, silver and wampum and jade and ideas have changed hands among Indian tribes from time immemorial. The resilience of the Indian spirit, the capacity to absorb and utilize the new and practical, has been repeatedly demonstrated. Indeed, the Indian's very survival in the face of swift and catastrophic change is irrevocable proof of his adaptability.

In the area of his religious life, as well as in the material world, the Indian has shown his ability to integrate his own ideals and spiritual satisfactions with the higher concepts of Christianity. The week-long camp meetings of the Creek Church members in Oklahoma, the all-day services of the Cherokees at their little churches in the hills; the great annual convocation of the Episcopalian Dakotas take the place of the tribal gatherings of ancient days and satisfy the longing of the people to work together. The great social ideal of giving, so deeply a part of Dakota culture, is enriched and given new meaning by the Christian ideal of sharing. It is not the fact of change that has attacked the spiritual resources of the Indian people, for they have met change during all the years of their racial life and built upon it. The frustration has come through the denial of their right to choose from the new world about them that which is meaningful and useful to their way of life.

They have been forced by relentless circumstance to abandon many of the great ideals that to them gave life its purpose. The breaking up of natural groups by the allotment system and by the early educational policies of the Federal government has among many tribes destroyed the warm relationships of clan and community. The government officials paid little attention to family or clan relationships. Sometimes this was because they knew nothing about such an organization of Indian society, but sometimes it was a deliberate attempt to break up these groups in the hope that white attitudes toward property and toward individual achievement might be more quickly accepted. Therefore, a group of Indian people who had lived and worked together for centuries as one close unit found themselves separated by wide acres, one allotted to a farm among strangers and another located on a farm where he became neighbor to a member of a clan that had been unfriendly.

The transforming, buoyant power of group influence that time and again down through the ages had held the people steady through devastating crises was undermined. The intense economic competition forced on them by their white conquerors violated the racial concepts of communal endeavor and ravaged their social organizations built up through centuries of cooperative experience. Their way of life disintegrated. Old customs no longer had meaning and the youth were taught in the government schools not to respect them. Leisure time, linked so completely with the religious life of the people, was left at loose ends when the old pageantry, the ceremonials, the ancient community religious expressions were destroyed. Often little was supplied in place of the old recreations and the whole fabric of life was weakened.

The general thinking of the times was that everything in white civilization was desirable, everything in Indian civilization inimical to progress; the conviction that the Indian personality was something that needed to be made over, re-created into the white pattern, dominated all dealing with Indians. In 1889 a Commissioner of Indian Affairs wrote in his annual report: "The Indians must conform to the white man's ways, peaceably if they will, forcibly if they must." That endeavor was ardently made for more than a century.

THE SEARCH FOR GOD

"I came not to destroy, but to fulfill," said Jesus, and his words apply as much to Indians as they did to the Hebrews of his day. Not through destruction of germs of spiritual truth but through their nourishment and enrichment does the Christian church best serve the Indian people. Young Indian Christians, torn between loyalty to their own traditions and a desire to be true to the teachings of their church, face many problems. Wise beyond measure is the religious teacher who sees in each outward expression of Indian ritual its inner grace of spiritual aspiration, and like St. Paul tells the story of the Unknown God whom they strive to know. A Christian Indian student relates her feeling as she watched her people dancing in the plaza:

It was a dance of thanksgiving, and my people believe it was given to them by the gods when they walked on earth with men. It was beautiful, like a prayer, and I know the dancers felt it was a prayer. As I watched I felt a deep spiritual gladness and a sense of unity with my people; and I felt a desire for them to know more completely the Christ whose teachings could give their spiritual strivings fulfillment.

"We were like the Hebrews of old," said a Christian Indian, "before we learned of Christianity. We had our laws and our teachings, but we did not know of the love of Jesus."

Almost ten years ago, in the shadow of distant mountains, the Arapahoes were holding a sun dance. On the last day of the ceremony they came to the Christian missionary.

"We have fasted," they told him, "for three days and three nights. There is much the Arapahoe does not know about God. We have prayed to him in the best way we know how, and we want you to offer up your prayers also in order that all good may come to our people."

Standing in front of the buffalo head, symbolic altar in that old, old ceremony, the missionary offered this prayer:

O God, who art the God of all nations and people, whom thy children the Arapahoes first knew as Ja-ba-ni-a-tha [The Unknown on High] and as Ba-hai-tet [Chief of All], but whom, through the teachings of thy blessed Son we have now come to know as Ha-sa-nau-nin [Our Father], bless all those who are gathered here to worship thee in an ancient ceremony; be present to us all as thou hast promised to be present to those who call upon thee; let these great days of prayer and fasting be holy days, not only for these men who have made their dance to thee, but for all the members of our tribe; bless the sick for whom at this time our prayers are especially offered; accept our grateful thanks for the benefits which thou hast bestowed upon us and those who are near and dear to us; let the light of thy Great Spirit shine in our hearts and minds that we may know thee as thou art and live as thou wouldst have us live; in all our weakness give us of thy power. And grant to us all the vision of thy being and thy beauty, that in the strength of it we may work without haste and without rest, through Jesus Christ our Lord. Amen.[1]

In these days when we understand more about the growth and development of human personality, we know that lives blossom more richly if roots sink deep in a past that is secure and respected. Indian youth do not look backward toward the old days. They know they cannot, in the tomorrow ahead, be the same kind

[1] Quoted from "Better Living for the Indian," issued by St. Michael's Mission, Ethete, Wyoming.

of Indians their ancestors were or live the same kind of lives their ancestors lived. But they need not cease to be Indian. No river returns to its source, yet all rivers must have a beginning. Indian youth, like the stream, must be fed from the source, gathering strength and wisdom from the tributaries of other cultures that flow into their lives, remaining to the end the same stream, but flowing ever wider, richer, more productive of life. Not by repudiating their heritage, but by using the strengths both of the past and the present, can they continue to grow strong and steadily.

4: GROWING UP IN TWO WORLDS

Turned by the wind goes the one I send yonder;
Yonder he goes who is whirled by the winds;
Goes, where the four hills of life and the four winds
    are standing;
There in the midst of the winds do I send him,
Into the midst of the winds, standing there.

—Omaha [1]

IT is difficult for an Indian to be objective about the
problems of being an Indian, even though one's skin
may be light enough to escape much of the backwash of
rejection America reserves for people of darker color.
Too many memories surge forward to crowd out ob-
jectivity. There is the memory, for instance, of the
Cherokee girl trying to find a place to live when she
came to Washington, D. C., to find work. She was
young, eager, neatly and smartly dressed, with a face
lovely as a dark glowing flower. "Are you Indian?" asked
the first landlady. "Oh, I couldn't possibly have an Indian girl live in my house." There is the Sunday morning at a church in the city. "The Indian students are to

[1] The Omaha Tribe, by Alice C. Fletcher and Francis La Flesche, p.
119. Washington, D. C., United States Bureau of American Ethnology,
1907. Used by permission.

sit over there," said the sweet-voiced lady, pointing out a dark obscure corner.

There is the Indian school, set like a jewel in the center of the wide, golden prairie. The campus is spacious, the buildings comfortable, the teachers kind and devoted. "Why don't you give the children schoolwork that requires real mental effort?" asked the visiting official. "You forget," replied the principal, "these are Indian children. We can't expect the same from them as from children of other races. We must always remember that they are Indians."

There is the dean of a college who is convinced that all Indians are lazy because in the years of his administration the three Indian students he had known were lazy. There is the head of a home economics department at a large university who accused the Indian girl in her class when theft occurred in her office because, as she said, her sister lived on the edge of an Indian reservation and knew that "all Indians steal." There are the Indian Service employees who are convinced that Indians do not love their children as white people do because they never fondle them; others who believe that all Indians are irresponsible. And there is the scene at the Navajo day school. The table was laid for tea and we were about to sit down, the white teacher, her Navajo assistant, and I, when a Navajo woman from a neighboring *hogan* came to the door. "Won't you come in and have tea with us?" asked the white teacher when their business was finished. "This is the first time in all my life," the woman said in Navajo to the assistant, "that a white person has treated me as an equal."

FAITH IN OURSELVES IS NECESSARY

It is a personal humiliation to discover that many white people working with Indians believe that they cling so stubbornly to their established way of life because of some innate racial defect; some character deficiency that renders them unable to attain the standards of white culture. Their social delinquencies, their excessive drinking, their shiftlessness, where these exist, are often seen as racial weaknesses rather than understood for what they actually are—symptoms of conflicts in individuals growing out of exactly the same kind of difficulties that cause conflicts in any human being.

We now know, for example, that a sense of inferiority may hold an individual in bondage more truly than irons or a prison. Pressures from all sides are exerted on Indian youth, pressures that cannot fail to injure his pride in his racial heritage and, by implication, weaken his confidence in his own ability. He sees his people almost universally overwhelmed by the most grievous poverty and pauperized by enforced dependency. His tribal assets, often even his own property, are in the control of other hands. His parents and neighbors have little to do with community planning or with plans for the future of their own children. All on his reservation are in a special status with regard to state and Federal laws. He cannot fail to know this is because Indians are not

considered competent to meet the demands of a sophis-
ticated white world.

The young Indian goes to school often to teachers
who consider him mentally inferior and so limit his
opportunities. He hears his customs condemned as "un-
civilized," "heathen," and "decadent" and is told that
the sooner he repudiates them the better. For years he
and his father before him have been encouraged to believe that "going back to the blanket"—living as his
people live, wearing the tribal costume—is the ultimate
in deterioration. He reads in pamphlets or books that
his religious dances and ceremonials are invitations to
immorality. He hears his people stigmatized as lazy,
dirty, cruel, and shiftless. He often meets discrimination
and prejudice.

THERE ARE NO SUPERIOR PEOPLE

Psychological tests have proved that Indians possess
the same mental capacities as whites. Scientists tell us
there are no superior races; that, while one individual in
a group may be more intelligent than a given individual
in another group, no whole group of people has greater
mental ability than any other. Indians, therefore, have
the same potential ability as the Chinese, the Negroes,
the Malays, or the Caucasians. It is opportunity and not
capacity that retards Indian progress.

There are many things that cloud Indian opportunity.
Indian youth today is forced to live in two worlds. The
old world, the aboriginal Indian world, grows more dim

and shadowy to each oncoming generation, but for long years to come it will continue to be a powerful reality in the lives of many young Indians. The threshold of the new world waits at the end of unfamiliar winding paths along which many have lost their way.

Indians, like all other people, get their beginning in the home. From birth until the ages of six or seven the Indian child is inculcated with the social ideals that make for good Indian life. His playmates, his relatives, the entire community reinforce the teachings of his family. During these compelling years, while the framework of his personality is being laid, the imprint of the Indian life-pattern is stamped indelibly on his heart and mind. Then he goes to school.

From the first day of school he begins to discover that many of the things his teachers do and teach him to do are in conflict with the teachings of his parents and community. This causes a breach in the emotional relationships between him and his parents. His confidence in their wisdom and his sense of security in his Indian world are shaken. As he goes farther along in school and discovers more and more in the white world that is at variance with Indian beliefs and practices, the psychological distance between him and his parents widens. When he hears Indian ways condemned, as he frequently does, his respect for his parents and all they represent is undermined. The realization that the dominant race does not consider the adults of his community competent to assume the responsibilities of adulthood lowers their status in his eyes and heightens his own sense of inadequacy. As a natural result he becomes antagonistic and questions both parental and group authority. This gap between the young Indian and his parents and community is particularly noticeable when Indian children have gone away to boarding school for long periods of time.

NO PLACE TO FIT IN

Through many generations of Indian youth, until as late as 1929, it was the practice of the Federal government—a practice vigorously opposed by many missionaries—to send Indian children away from their homes to distant boarding schools. The idea back of this policy was that if Indian children were kept out of the Indian environment long enough and educated in white ways assiduously enough, they would forget their Indian background and become "civilized" by taking on white ways. The implication was that upon graduation the Indian student would be accepted by the white world. He seldom was. A recent study carried out by the Education Division of the Indian Office revealed that an overwhelming percentage of Indian boarding school graduates, with the exception of students from California and Oklahoma, had returned to their homes.

Unable to find employment in white communities or unable to achieve a satisfactory adjustment, the Indian student came back to a community that had remained static while he had grown in skills and knowledge. Often he returned to a community that was so beaten down by poverty and dependency that idleness and lethargy were its dominant characteristics. Too frequently he found an overcrowded, poverty-stricken home that offered him no opportunity to use the skills he had learned at school. Always he came back a stranger who had to win new acceptance from his group. Many had missed the initiation ceremonies and other rites that might have given them unity with their group. They were clumsy at Indian ways. Often they felt superior. And sometimes they assumed an air of superiority to hide their awful feeling of belonging nowhere. This only served to alienate them further. The old men, who are always the leaders in Indian communities, did not hesitate to say that school had spoiled them and that they could not fit into the Indian pattern.

The presence of a growing body of frustrated young people rapidly accelerated the social and cultural disorganization already apparent on many reservations. The old Indian sanctions and social controls were destroyed and no white equivalents replaced them. Immeasurable damage was done the communities. Maladjustment and insecurity have been cumulative from one generation to another, for parents who are themselves insecure and uncertain have been unable to give their children certainty. Chaos and disorder have multiplied.

Such difficulties as these are not easily overcome. It will take a clear understanding of what causes them and the cooperation of home, school, and church to remedy this situation.

THE INDIAN HOME, THE CENTER OF EMPHASIS IN EDUCATION

Experience revealed that the boarding school was not meeting Indian needs. The Indian graduate was not being taken into white communities nor could he provide the Indian community with the leadership needed in the struggle for adaptation. If reservation life was to become productive and satisfying, the Indian home must become the center of approach. Beginning in 1929 and continuing through today, the main emphasis of Federal Indian education has been on day schools and public schools that enable Indian children to live at home and share in a school experience embracing all the members of the family.

The ideal of the present day school program on Indian reservations is to bring the entire Indian community into the life of the school. Adults as well as children are included in school activities. Women come for classes in homemaking and child care. They use the school kitchens for canning and preserving food, the school sewing rooms for repairing and making clothes for their families. The men come to the school shops to build furniture for their homes, to repair their farm machinery, and they borrow tools to carry home to repair the sagging doorstep or the broken window. In communities where water is precious and difficult to obtain, the school provides laundry and bathing facilities. There is a meeting place for social affairs, and gradually libra-

ries are being developed. Teachers are sought who are
sensitive to community needs and who are able to give
guidance to the adults as well as the children. Daily the
Indian child, just as every other American child, carries
home from the school the new knowledge he has gained
and thus the home grows as the child grows.

Responsibility for the education of Indian youth is
assumed by three separate agencies—the Federal government, the various states in which Indians live, and the
church. In 1944 there were 82,265 Indian children between the ages of six and eighteen attending schools in
the United States. Of this number, 35,031 were in public
schools, 7,068 were enrolled in the various mission
schools throughout the Indian country, and the re-
mainder were in the schools operated by the Federal
Indian Service. There were during that same year 12,000
Indian children not enrolled in any school, largely because no school facilities existed for them.[1]

SCHOOLS OF THE INDIAN SERVICE

The Federal Indian schools are of three types: the
community day school where the students come daily
from their homes; the reservation boarding school where
the students live at the school during week days but
spend week-ends and holidays at home; and the non-
reservation boarding schools usually located considerable
distances from the Indian country. Enrollment in the

[1] Figures taken from reports of Education Division, Office of Indian
Affairs.

non-reservation boarding schools has for more than a decade been limited to the advanced students who want specialized vocational training to fit them for employment in the industrial world, and to that rather large group of Indian children who are in need of institutional care.

Haskell Institute, at Lawrence, Kansas, is one of nine large non-reservation boarding schools of high school level. Each of these has a usual enrollment of around six hundred students. In addition to the regular academic high school course, Haskell Institute offers trades such as carpentry, welding, baking, cooking, dressmaking, homemaking, and a two-year postgraduate commercial course. Graduates of the commercial department find employment mainly in the Indian Service as clerks and stenographers, but they are increasingly finding similar jobs in many cities and towns of America. Chilocco Indian School in Oklahoma specializes in agriculture. Here students acquire, under guidance, actual experience in running a farm and raising livestock. Sherman Institute in California concentrates primarily on preparing Indian youth for employment in the industrial centers of the West coast, but this school also, in common with all other Federal Indian schools, gives thorough training in agriculture and homemaking.

The government recognizes a twofold task in its educational program for Indians: one, making effective their citizenship by encouraging their active participation in local programs of welfare and education; and the

other, teaching Indian youth to develop to the highest
degree possible the resources of the communities in
which they live. More and more Indian reservations are
coming to be simply American rural communities settled by a people of different racial and cultural background who are living there because that is where they
prefer to live. They prefer it for the same reason that
a Californian prefers to live in California or a native of
Tennessee likes Tennessee best—it is home, the place
where from childhood they have known life's dearest
satisfactions; and it is the place where their friends and
loved ones are.

The great objective of the Federal community schools
is to strengthen American Indian life by making these
rural Indian communities more productive economically
and by giving the young people the kind of education
that will inspire them to meet their problems with
greater imagination and courage. The schools differ
widely in different areas of the country for they are patterned on the agricultural needs and the occupational
opportunities of the region. On the Pine Ridge Reservation in South Dakota, for example, cattle offer the
best economic hope because of the type of land available. At the Oglala Community High School in this
area the school program is built around a herd of more
than eight hundred beef cattle. The boys of the school
may belong to a cattle association and may earn cattle
to start themselves in the livestock business when they
are ready to leave school. At Carson Agency, Nevada,

pupils still enrolled in school operate actual business enterprises under the supervision of their instructors and the activities of the enterprise form the basis of much of their classroom work. In one year there were one hundred and forty-eight student enterprises in operation at this school. The young people contract with the school for seed, land, and livestock and pay for them from the proceeds of their labor. They sell their own produce and use what they earn above the original investment in whatever way they decide best.

While the program of the community schools is definitely related to the area in which the students live, an attempt is made to give each Indian youth an education broad enough to enable him to have some choice as to where he will live and the occupation he will follow when his school days are over. The hope is that his education will have been so effective that he can succeed either on the reservation, if that is where he elects to stay, or out in the white world, if this is his choice.

"If we can train Indian young people to do one thing superlatively well," says Willard Beatty, Director of Education for the Indian Service, "and give them an introduction to a number of other skills, they should then have self-confidence enough to succeed wherever they may be."

PUBLIC SCHOOLS

Almost half the total Indian school population is in the public schools of the United States. But for approximately forty-four per cent of the Indian population no public schools are available. In order to facilitate greater public school attendance, the Indian Service negotiates contracts with the states of California, Washington, Minnesota, Wisconsin, and, in a limited way, with Arizona to pay the states for providing educational and welfare services to Indians living on non-taxable lands within these states. Many Indian parents, and particularly mixed-blood parents, realizing that assimilation with white ways of life is as inevitable as the passing of the seasons, prefer to hasten the process by having their children attend schools with the white children of the communities in which they live.

"It will be easier for them," one thoughtful Indian father explained, "when the time comes to make their living in competition with the white man if our children have learned to know their ways from childhood. They can do this best on the playgrounds and in the classrooms of the school."

SCHOOLS OF THE CHURCH

Mission schools were the first to offer educational opportunities to Indians, long before there were Federal schools. Indeed, it was the Christian churches of America that alone carried the full responsibility for the education of Indians for more than three hundred years (between the years 1560 and 1880). The example of the mission schools, their gratifying results in the advancement and progress of the Indian communities and in the training of Indian leadership, together with the tireless efforts of the missionaries in the Indians' behalf, finally wakened the American people to the need of providing for the education of the American Indian and led to the establishment of the Federal Indian schools. As the Federal government assumed more and more responsibility for the education of Indians, and as public school facilities for them increased, the mission schools decreased in numbers until today less than one-tenth of the Indian school population is attending mission schools.

Bacone College, at Bacone, Oklahoma, just outside the city limits of Muskogee, is a junior college for Indians, operated by the two home mission societies of the Northern Baptist Convention. Bacone also maintains a high school, and an elementary school for the children of the Murrow Orphanage is under the same management. One of the great contributions of Bacone College is the training of Indian teachers for the small Indian public schools of Oklahoma. The elementary school serves to provide practice teaching experience for these young student teachers. The Ganado Mission at Ganado, Arizona, maintained by the Board of National Missions of the Presbyterian Church in the United States of America, operates both a high school and an elementary school for Navajos; and a fully accredited school of nursing, open to women of all tribes and to Spanish Americans, is maintained in connection with the Ganado medical center. The Navajo Methodist Mission School at Farmington, New Mexico, also offers high school work to Navajo boys and girls. This school specializes in agriculture and homemaking, in addition to preparing young Navajos for leadership among their own people. St. Mary's Episcopal School for girls is a high school for Indian girls of North and South Dakota. Tucson Training School at Tucson, Arizona, has both primary and high school work and many students go on to the University of Arizona.

There are a number of mission schools offering educational work below the high school level. Dwight Mission for the Cherokees of Oklahoma, under the auspices of the Presbyterian Church in the U. S. A., is a school of this type, as is the school operated by the Evangelical and Reformed Church at Neilsville, Wisconsin, for Winnebago boys and girls.

Believing that work and play together promote the understanding and fellowship desirable among people of all groups, the churches were among the first to transfer their Indian students from the segregated mission boarding schools into neighboring public schools wherever this was feasible. The boarding school plants were then converted into Christian boarding homes for Indian children who could not live at home. The important function of such boarding homes cannot be overestimated. Many Indian children live too far from the school to go back and forth daily, or live in areas where the winter is too severe for daily bus travel to the school. These students live at the mission dormitories during the school week, returning to their homes for the week-ends. Other pupils, who cannot live at home because of illness there or for other reasons, and orphans without permanent homes have found in the mission boarding home a sanctuary and an opportunity. These homes endeavor to provide a normal homelike atmosphere for the Indian children and to teach them how to build Christian homes of their own when the time comes.

The Oklahoma Presbyterian College at Durant, Oklahoma, under the auspices of the Presbyterian Church in the United States, is an example of the modern mission boarding home. This institution is providing a Christian home and Christian education for young Indian women of Oklahoma who are attending both the Southeastern State College at Durant and the city high school. Graduates of Southeastern who have spent four years and sometimes longer as residents of Oklahoma Presbyterian College are now making profound and lasting contributions to Indian advancement as teachers in the Indian Service and in public schools, as social workers, and as housewives and mothers. St. Elizabeth's at Wakpala, South Dakota, under the Protestant Episcopal Church is another example of the mission boarding home. For many years the Reformed Church in America provided this type of service for boys and girls of the Winnebago reservation who were attending the public high school in the town of Winnebago, Nebraska.

The mission school program usually is similar to that of the government schools in that the training offered is practical in nature. All these schools have courses in homemaking and most of them offer some work in agriculture and in the trades. Practically all of them provide college preparatory work. But the mission schools have as their first objective the training of Indian children in the Christian way of life. To this end they each place strong emphasis on the ideal of Christian service. Their purpose is to teach Indian youth not only how to make a living but also how to live worthily as Christian citizens.

One of the most significant educational projects undertaken by the churches is the employment of religious work directors to serve in six of the larger non-reservation boarding schools of the Indian Service. This project represents an example of successful cooperation between the government and the churches, as well as cooperation among the various denominations. Fifteen denominations have united through the Home Missions Council of North America and jointly provide funds for the salaries of workers at Haskell Institute, Lawrence, Kansas; Chilocco Indian School, Chilocco, Oklahoma; Flandreau Indian School, Flandreau, South Dakota; Chemawa Indian School, Chemawa, Oregon; Phoenix Indian School, Phoenix, Arizona; Albuquerque Indian School, Albuquerque, New Mexico; and Sherman Institute, Riverside, California. These directors, trained in religious education and in recreation and guidance, have proved to be extremely useful additions to the staff of the government schools where they are at work. They are helping the students of these institutions in different ways to make their adjustments to what, for many, is a new way of life.

SOME PROBLEMS OF ADJUSTMENT

The new policy of allowing the Indian child to grow up in his home environment, under the direct influence and guidance of his parents and his community, has now been in operation for about fourteen years, and there is considerable evidence that this has tended to promote greater harmony and understanding between the older and the younger generations. But all the misunderstandings and difficulties have not, of course, been so easily resolved. There are still profound adjustments to be made in the difficult process of assimilating an old and a new culture.

For example, what is an energetic, ambitious, and intelligent Indian youth to do when he is eager to introduce new methods of agriculture to his group? Leadership belongs to the old men, according to Indian tradition. Must he usurp their prerogatives and thus put both them and himself in a false position? Or must he wait until he, too, becomes an old man to put his ideas into operation?

What of the young man who has been thoroughly indoctrinated in those deeply implanted Indian ideals of hospitality and generosity? The schools have taught him to get ahead, to accumulate goods and property against a rainy day. Can he do this if he follows Indian custom? Indian generosity and hospitality become a liability under the American economic system. Must he betray those ideals that bring him greater recognition from his group than money does?

Peter belongs to a tribe whose traditions of marriage require him to live with his wife's family and give to her people his economic support. The American way teaches him to take a house and farmland for himself and work only for his own family, to let his wife's family stand on their own feet. But his wife has been trained from infancy to implicit paternal obedience. What is Peter to do? Can he break all family ties to follow the American pattern of individualism?

Just as bewildering is the dilemma of the young man who has left the Indian community to make his way in the white world. Neither the Indian community nor the Federal government has clearly defined his status. Does he still belong to the Indian community or to the white world? Nobody knows. If he gets into difficulty in a white community, the authorities there, confused as to their responsibilities, frequently send him back to the reservation for the "government to take care of." If jobs get scarce, he is the first to lose his job, not always because of race prejudice, but because the white unemployed of the community have to be supported and it is the employer's belief that Indians can return to the reservation where the government will provide for their needs. On the other hand, more and more Indian communities are coming to feel that those Indians who leave the group for an extended time are not entitled to share in the group benefits. Recently a young Indian who had been away from his village for several years applied for his share of the tribal funds that were then being distributed among the group members. The village decided that since he was not there to carry his share of responsibility for the group welfare and upkeep of the village, he could not share in the village resources.

The facts that a break with old Indian ways is inevitable and that Indian youth must learn to live in a white world, following more and more the white way of life, do not make the problems created thereby any less acute. The task confronting those agencies concerned with Indian education is to help Indian youth understand the forces at work in their lives and to help them find the most effective ways to meet these forces. We have not often done this. Instead we have frequently condemned as weaklings young Indians who have reacted to conditions that they face exactly as other human beings react in like circumstances. When they are deprived of secure relationships with their own people, rejected by the white group, denied adult responsibilities, often without opportunity to use their training, ill fed, reared in overcrowded homes, Indian youth have responded just as youth of all races who face the same frustrations. Some manage to overcome these handicaps. Many do not. These leave school. Or they drink to excess. They change their jobs frequently. They flout paternal control. They spend their money foolishly. They get into sex difficulties. They sink into idleness and apathy. In such ways as these some seek to escape from their difficulties. Others find friends whose counsel is wise, and plans are worked out to overcome the many handicaps.

PEOPLE MUST PLAY

Added to these basic factors, which make it difficult for young Indians to grow up normally, is the extreme poverty of many Indian reservations. As in other poverty-stricken rural communities in the United States, the resources for wholesome recreation are extremely limited. In the old life recreation was an integral part of the Indian pattern, tied closely into the religious and work life of the people. But where the old customs have disappeared, no forms of organized recreation have been built up to replace those that have vanished. Often only the less constructive forms of recreation, such as gambling, drinking, and loafing, have remained to take their place. The schools on the reservations and the government agencies have all too often neglected this phase of Indian life, and the Indian churches for many long years frowned on most forms of play for the youth of the community.

Many of the early government employees and missionaries, brought up in a rigid and difficult school of life, did not understand the value of wholesome recreation as we view it today. And in the early Indian life, pageantry and many other forms of recreational activity were connected with their religious expressions. It was natural, therefore, that the early Indian converts to Christianity should feel that play in many of the forms we know it savored of the old pagan practices and was to be shunned. Even football was fought by Indian

Christians in some localities as an unsuitable activity to be sponsored by a mission school.

Indian homes, frequently overcrowded and uninviting, offer little room for home entertainment and force many Indian girls to meet their men acquaintances outside the home and away from the restraining influence of their elders. This is completely outside the Indian pattern and leads to further breakdown in social disciplines and still greater misunderstanding between the young and the old.

Despite these very real difficulties, many young Indians are finding ways to create a home and standards of living that are creditable. With the helpful understanding of better privileged people, this progress can be hastened.

NOBODY LIKES TO BE LABELED

One of the most perplexing difficulties young Indians have to face is the stereotyped notions that many white people have of how an Indian ought to behave. Such notions vary as the white man's experience with Indians may vary, but in every case they restrict the Indian's right to consideration on his own merits as an individual. "We cannot expect too much of the Indian individually or collectively," some white workers among Indians believe, forgetting that all human beings usually try to live up to what is expected of them. "That is pretty good—for an Indian," is another version of the same idea heard frequently. This attitude also robs Indian youth of the challenge to higher achievement.

"I have not told anyone here that I am an Indian," said a mixed-blood Indian student when I visited his college. "It isn't that I am ashamed of being Indian, for I'm not. But I want to be responsible for my own mistakes, and I want to make my own way without anything being added to me or taken away from me because of my race. I don't want to be labeled." This feeling of wanting to be considered simply as human beings, free of the sentimental or derogatory notions about Indians, is strong among many Indian youth.

Not long ago four Indian girls entered nursing school in a large midwestern hospital. Three of them left not long afterward. When I went to discover the cause, I found that the Director of Nurses had told them, "I didn't want to accept you Indian girls but my superior talked me into it. I know from experience the shortcomings of your people. I want you to know you will be watched closely and if I see any of those weaknesses in you, I shall dismiss you." The one girl who stayed on said, "I was determined to prove to her that all Indians were not like she thought. So I put up with everything and I'm going to stick it out until graduation." But the other three could not endure the doubt and skepticism. "I couldn't stand feeling that I was watched all the time and that every mistake I made was chalked up against the whole race," one gave as her reason for leaving. It is never pleasant to be labeled, and when the label is the result of someone's prejudice or of an unfair generalization, the indignity is even harder to endure.

THERE ARE REASONS WHY PEOPLE BEHAVE AS THEY DO

Often the unfriendly ideas about Indians grow up out of misunderstanding of Indian ways of looking at life. "Indian children are different," I have heard teachers say. "They are sullen; and won't speak up in class." "They won't lift up their heads and look you straight in the eye." The teacher who thus condemns the Indian child is judging him by the only standards of behavior she knows, the white standards, but in this she may be doing the child serious injustice. When he does not respond in class, he may be behaving as any polite Indian child should behave. Well-brought-up Indian children keep silent in the presence of adults. Moreover, to make oneself conspicuous by standing out above the rest of the group through too much talking in class is not good Indian conduct. In the white pattern of behavior, failure to look one straight in the eye implies some devious trait of character. But in the Indian pattern it is, among some tribes, most impolite to stare straight into the eyes of another person for this is too prying, too inquisitive.

If such surface customs are so easily misunderstood, how much easier it must be to misunderstand the deeper, underlying motivations and drives that determine Indian conduct! The lack of ambition, for example, so often deplored in Indians can generally be explained by difference in wants and incentives.

Material prosperity, the accumulation of money in the

bank or ownership of things, has not yet entered the
Indian group concept as desirable or worth the enslave-
ment it costs. While here and there individuals are finding satisfactions in the white pattern of living, many of
the wants of Indians are extremely simple; their deepest
values are still spiritual. The close family circle, the un-
hurried existence with time for dreaming, the warm support of clan and tribal group, the joy of song and dance,
still call to them more strongly than the accumulation of
goods.

The good man in Indian culture, the man whom Indian youth is taught to emulate, may differ somewhat in
characteristics among the different tribes, but he is seldom the rich man of the village. He is the man who is
generous, who makes many sacrifices for the people. He
must have great dignity and a good heart. He must practise good social behavior as the tribe knows it. But he
does not need to have money or the largest house in the
village or to be a success in a job. He must not be quar-
relsome, he must not put his own interests ahead of the
group, he must have spiritual power and wisdom, but he
need not be what the white man calls a "hard worker."

This ideal has tremendous influence on the things
many Indian youth of today consider worth striving for
and explains what many white teachers have deplored
as lack of ambition. An Indian boy leaves a good job in
the city to return to the reservation where idleness, poverty, and want will be daily companions. It is easy to say
as we look at him, "It does no good to educate an In-

dian." It is easy to condemn him as shiftless and lazy if we do not understand that for him security and satisfaction exist in something he did not find in a good job and a chance to save money for the future. If we are to judge Indians fairly, we must try to understand why they act as they do.

FALSE NOTIONS

Frequently unfair notions of Indians grow out of lack of knowledge of true conditions. In a state with a large Indian population, it was proposed that Indian children attend the public schools. The white people of the community objected in the honest belief that Indians were all diseased and would infect the white children. The wise state official, whose function it was to arrange the public school attendance, handled the objection by insisting that both white and Indian children be examined by a competent physician. The examination revealed that the white children of the community were even more in need of medical care than were the Indians.

An obstacle to the placement of Indians in training situations under the National Youth Administration, according to an official of that organization, was the widespread notion that Indians were different and needed special handling. Indian young people realize the handicap this kind of thinking can be to them and more and more they want to be free of it.

"What we want more than anything else in the

world," said one group of Indian girls, speaking for all Indian young people with whom they were acquainted, "is not to be different. We don't want to be set apart. We want to be just people."

Indians suffer from the same kind of limitations in understanding white people. They also have preconceived notions of how all white men will behave. They look at the white man out of the windows of their own experiences. They, too, make wrong interpretations. All white men are viewed by some Indians with suspicion and fear. They are determined, so these Indians believe, to put something over on Indians if they can. Indian children are still sometimes frightened into good behavior by the threat that the white man will come to take them away, just as the pioneer white mother used to quiet her youngsters with the threat of the Indian warrior.

Often Indians are super-critical because of some past experiences they have had, and read into situations prejudices that do not actually exist. Many find it almost impossible not to look for and expect discrimination. Often there is a tendency to lay all blame for everything wrong that happens to them to the treachery and guile of the white man. Out of this attitude, there has grown up among some Indians a kind of persecution complex. They carry a permanent chip on their shoulders. If their plans go awry, if there are errors or failures, it is due to the nefarious white man. If they lose their jobs or fail to achieve promotion, it is, in the minds of such individuals, due to the unfairness of their white employers. They are without the courage to face their own shortcomings, forgetting that white people also lose their jobs and that white people also fail to secure promotion. Such Indians are unable to look at life realistically. It is easier to blame the other fellow for prejudice than to do a piece of critical self-searching. This unwholesome attitude is more crippling to the freedom of the spirit than any other one thing. Where it prevails, there can be no creative, adventurous endeavor. It is a sickness that destroys, for it prevents the self-analysis that is the basis of growth.

Indians need to be helped to understand and to trust the good intentions of white people fully as much as white people need to be helped to understand the Indians. They need to give white people whose intentions toward them are good a chance to express their friendliness. If the two races are ever to meet on a common ground of friendship and understanding, Indians must cover a part of the distance.

LEARNING ABOUT WHITE LIFE THE HARD WAY

Unfortunately, Indians in many sections of the United States have little chance to know the better class of white people. We are likely to think that on the reservations Indians are in contact with the intellectuals of the white group. They go to school to white teachers, they take supervision from white extension agents, they are ministered to by white missionaries, they buy their goods from a white trader. Surely, we say, this is a good class of white people to know and to emulate.

But Indians do not usually have an opportunity to know these people well enough to want to be like them. The private thoughts, the home lives, the hopes and aspirations that are in reality the central core of white civilization, are often unknown to Indians. There are few genuine friendships between members of the two groups. All of these people do deal with Indians every day in a professional capacity, but they seldom enter into Indian life nor do Indians enter their life. There is rarely fraternity based on equality. The barrier may be partly language, only sometimes race. Chiefly it is poverty and a difference in ways of looking at life. There is a gulf a thousand miles deep between the daughter of the white superintendent of an Indian reservation and the daughter of Sam Spotted Deer, the typical reservation full-blood Indian.

The missionary has been the staunchest and truest friend the Indian has had in all his long history of white relationships. Yet sometimes even the missionary goes to the Indians as a messenger bringing light instead of seeking to be a friend to share difficulties and joys. Many times he, like the agents and teachers, has failed to look upon the Indian as a personal friend. Because of all of this, Indians often feel that the white workers have no genuine interest in them as human beings; and because of this Indians have little chance to know the best and greatest satisfactions in white life intimately enough to

want to copy them. And the substantial white residents
of the community live apart from the Indians. If they
think of them at all, it is often with pity or contempt.
They are more likely to be merely indifferent and wholly
unconcerned.

"If Indians were to attend the public schools with
white children," we sometimes hear, "this unfortunate
separation would not occur, for then Indians and whites
could grow up together and, through long and intimate
knowledge, understand each other." Unhappily this is
not always the way it works out. The younger children
going to school together do play in harmony and feel
none of those barriers that separate the adults. But along
about adolescence, when the Indian youth needs acceptance and security perhaps more than at any other time,
the barriers begin to loom strongly in the forefront; and
often the full-blood group is ostracized. Many Indians
drop out of the public school rather than face this social
rejection.

The white people who most frequently solicit Indian
friendship and who are willing to fraternize with them
in those localities where there is prejudice, are the out-
casts of white society—the gambler, the prostitute, the
bootlegger, the adventurer, the tough farmhand and
cowboy who come to the towns on the border of the
reservations on Saturday night for their weekly drunk.
Even these more often than not are out to exploit Indians rather than befriend them. Denied the opportunity really to know and become a part of the best of

white civilization, Indians are often forced to accept its most destructive elements.

There are localities where this is not a true picture. In Oklahoma, for example, and in some other parts of the United States, Indians and whites intermingle freely, and Indians are accepted on terms of complete equality. They are often elected to the most important offices of the state and county. They hold responsible positions in business enterprises in the cities and towns; they are on the faculties of the schools and colleges and marry into the best white families of the community.

WHERE DOES DEMOCRACY BEGIN FOR INDIANS?

But Indians have suffered most because they have been deprived of the responsibilities of adulthood. The trend of the present administration is to give Indians greater control over their own affairs. But there is room for still greater progress in this direction. From childhood to old age many Indians are kept in a protected, childlike status. They live on reservations run for them, not by them. They send their children to schools for which they are allowed to assume no important responsibility or direction. They receive medical care in hospitals to which they contribute neither labor nor funds. They work in cattle industries and community gardens planned, initiated, and managed by government employees. They attend churches run for them. In many cases their tribal assets are managed for them by the Indian Office; their own wishes are often ignored. They are served by Indian Office officials whom they have no voice in choosing. Their trust funds are controlled and spent at the discretion of some Indian Service employee, not at their own.

This situation, so un-American in principle, grows out of the Indians' wardship status and is the result of the Federal government's effort to exercise the responsibilities of guardianship. It is perpetuated by a belief that Indians can and will do nothing for themselves except under the supervision of some paid official. For over one hundred years practically all their thinking has been done for them by a benevolent government and a willing church. Even the simplest responsibilities have often been eased from their shoulders. They have not been trained to manage their own affairs.

Recently I heard of a group of women in an Indian community who joined together in a plan to provide hot lunches for their children at the local school. Each contributed food and alternated during the school days in preparing the lunch. All went well until the reservation superintendent came along.

"Why didn't you tell me you needed hot lunches for the school?" said he. "I can get you plenty of W.P.A. funds to take care of the whole thing." And another effort at self-help quietly folded up.

It is this kind of system, practised so long and so thoroughly, that has often destroyed any stimulus to Indian initiative. For over a century Indians have been slowly developing a deepening sense of dependence on the Federal government, until many have lost the power to believe in their own ability to stand alone.

We have believed in the principle of learning by trial and error for every other American, but not for the American Indian. They do not govern themselves without Federal supervision because the Federal government is afraid they will be exploited. They are not allowed to handle their own trust money because the Federal government is afraid they will make mistakes in the use of it. Yet all around them every day, Indians see other people of other races running into difficulties in attempting to govern themselves, and spending their money foolishly or wisely as they choose.

Indians borrow money from the Indian Office credit fund to purchase stock. They work hard and repay the debt in full with money earned by running their cattle business well. But when the loan is paid, they still cannot sell these cattle as any other citizen might. They must first secure permission from the Indian Office.

Indians have money in the agency of the Office of Indian Affairs, money that belongs to them personally from leasing or from mineral resources on trust property. They must get permission from the Indian Office to spend these funds. Many Indians feel humiliated and degraded at having to ask some other person for the right to spend their own funds, and to have to explain in detail how the money is to be spent. They spend much of their energy and time in thinking up ways and means to inveigle their own money out of the hands of the Indian Office. Age has nothing to do with this guardianship, and sometimes neither does competency. I read only recently of an Indian man who had worked long and well enough to retire on a pension but who still had to submit a budget to the Indian Office before he could get his own money released for his use. I know a man who is in middle age, employed and supporting his family, who was refused his own funds under the care of the Indian Office on the ground that he had a job and shouldn't be needing it.

While there are many individuals who still need protection from exploitation, it is obvious that there is desperate need for a more liberal interpretation of wardship status if Indians are to grow in the way that is the birthright of every other American citizen.

There is a story I can tell that has a happy ending. A state with a large Indian population established a public school in an Indian community. "Do you think those Indians can run their school?" was the skeptical query of several government and county officials when the state department of education proposed a school board for them as for every other public school district. But the state official who believed democracy was intended to function for all people insisted, and an Indian school board was elected. The first year they ran into trouble. One member of the board was suspected of graft and there was trouble with the teaching staff. Immediately there was a clamor to dissolve the school board on the ground the Indians had demonstrated they were not yet ready to manage such complicated government as a public school. But the state official was stubborn, and he believed in Indian ability.

"They have the same right," he said, "to work themselves out of this difficulty as any other people in a democracy. They are not the first community to elect crooked officers. And they won't be the last. They shouldn't be condemned for their first mistake."

Events proved his confidence to be justified. At the next election the undesirable board member was not reelected. The trouble was ironed out and, though it is now several years since that date, the public school is operating smoothly under Indian management.

A NEW PERSPECTIVE

Indian youth, moving today out beyond the borders of an isolated community into the life of America, is discovering that Indians are not the first people to be supplanted by a stronger group, nor yet the last. He is learning that Indians in America have fared far better than have subjugated people of many other lands, before them and after. He is finding that poverty with its attendant evils is not an Indian characteristic, for he sees others as poverty-stricken as the poorest of his people. He sees that other races in America are forced to endure even greater prejudice and scorn.

Others, besides Indians, he finds, have also owned land and lost it, and built a new life just the same. The boy who works beside him at the factory is the son of a homesteader who also received government land, and later sold it. The white migrant family he met at the beet fields once owned a farm, they told him, but lost it to the bank because they could not pay the mortgage on it. Land holdings have often been wiped out by war or depressions.

Indian youth, in numbers that run to more than twenty thousand, are fighting in the armed forces all over the world. They send letters home from far places —Persia, India, Puerto Rico, Australia, and England. These letters tell of people without freedom, of poverty and disease and bravery. Many more thousands of Indians are working in the mines, cities, and factories of America. Here they meet refugees from war-torn countries who must begin life all over again in America without the help of a benevolent government. They meet American-born Japanese who have been interned because of their race, whose farms and businesses were sacrificed by war. It is revealing to discover that these dispossessed people are not wasting precious time in dreaming of past glories, that they do not yield to self-pity or fruitless antagonisms, that they are asking only for a chance to work.

Never again will those Indians who have been given this insight into the problems of others see their own problem in its old narrow framework. For these, the prison house of self-interest, which segregation always builds up, has been shattered by a new and deepening understanding of the common needs of all people. It is to their everlasting glory that Indians, denied self-rule, have so willingly gone out to fight a war to insure self-rule for others. In these times that demand that no man think first of himself, Indians have forgotten self and stood forth in comradeship with all those who believe that the preservation of freedom and human equality are worth dying for.

5: WHO SHALL LEAD THE PEOPLE?

When I hear the old men
Telling of the heroes
Telling of the great deeds of ancient days,
When I hear that telling
Then I think within me
I, too, am one of these.

—Sioux [1]

PETALASHARO was an early leader of the Pawnees. Highly gifted, they picture him, master of
golden words, and of a nature deeply spiritual; gay and
courageous, too, and very skillful. The Pawnees say it
was inevitable he should become a tribal chief.

For many years, so the legend goes, Petalasharo
watched the ritual to the Morning Star with troubled
heart, pondering in silence the nature of a god to whom
the sacrifice of a captive virgin was required. Down
through long years, when the season was at hand, the
ceremony had been carried through. First, the priests
would choose the war party, then purify and bless them
with ritual, and send them forth into an enemy camp to
capture the maiden for the Morning Star. And then

[1] American Rhythm, by Mary Austin, p. 113. Boston, Houghton
Mifflin Co., 1930. Used by permission.

came the ritual of sacrifice. Death and calamity were sure, so the tribe believed, if they failed to propitiate the sullen god.

When Petalasharo was in his middle years and a ruling chieftain, a young Comanche girl was captured for the sacrifice. But as the priests led her to the altar Petalasharo overtook them on his racing horse, cut the thongs that bound her, and rode with her across the prairie to her home and safety. Stunned, the people waited in terror for the vengeance that surely would befall them. Nothing happened. And when Petalasharo returned unharmed to offer his own life in forfeit, the people ruled henceforward to discontinue the sacrifice.

Thus have the Indian people, as have all people, moved forward step by slow step through the wisdom and the vision and the courage of their great men.

THERE HAVE ALWAYS BEEN INDIAN LEADERS

Among the ancient Indians, as everywhere among all people, there was leadership in many fields and at many levels—in war, in hunting, in the planting of the fields, in healing, and in the sacred matters of the spirit. It was not an inherited leadership, as many have supposed. Rather among most of the tribes it was a leadership spontaneous and volatile, flowing directly from the will of the people.

The Apache *nanta*, for example, was followed by his people because they believed in his ability and courage. His followers were those who felt that under his guidance were to be found their best chances for the good life. They listened to his counsel, but they were free to follow it as they chose, and free to leave him when they no longer felt confidence in his wisdom.

Among the Pueblos this democratic ideal is carried even further. To this day it is undignified to seek public office in the affairs of the Pueblo. And he who attempts on his own initiative to gather power and influence into his own hands is censured by the people. But tradition requires that whoever is called must serve the people at whatever personal sacrifice. Francis Parkman, writing of the Indians of the plains, says:

Each village has a chief who is honored and obeyed only in so far as his personal qualities command respect and fear; sometimes his authority is little short of absolute, and his fame and influence reach beyond his own village so that the whole band is ready to acknowledge him as their head. This was, a few years hence, the case with the Ogillalah. Courage, address, enterprise may raise any warrior to the highest rank, especially if he be the son of a former chief or member of a numerous family to support him and avenge his quarrels; but when he has reached the dignity of chief, and the old men and warriors, by a peculiar ceremony, have formally installed him, let it not be imagined that he assumes any of the outward signs of rank and honor. He knows too well on how frail a tenure he holds his station.[1]

In this manner the Indians governed themselves until reservation life destroyed the old ways. Their leaders

[1] From *The Oregon Trail,* by Francis Parkman, reprinted by permission of Farrar & Rinehart, Inc., publishers.

were numerous and often achieved greatness in many lines of endeavor. Greatness did not come from one's effort alone. Every boy of the plains, every boy from tribes east and west, was taught to seek a vision at entrance to manhood. This vision would give him power and direction for all the days of his life. His boyhood was dedicated to preparation for his great quest. Cleanness and faith were his armor as he went alone into the mountains to fast and pray until the vision came. Sometimes none came, and then the man would be poor indeed. Sometimes to the favored the vision came unsought. Black Elk was nine years of age when his great vision came, unasked—a vision so strong, so beautiful that all his life long he forgot no part of it; and all his long life was filled with sorrow because he had failed to carry the vision's full message to his people.

"I did not depend upon the great vision as I should have done," he admitted sadly in his old age. "It is hard to follow one great vision in this world of darkness and changing shadows. Among these shadows men get lost." [1]

Washakie, Crazy Horse, Sequoyah, Pope, Sacajawea, Chief Joseph, Samson Occum—these are names that belong in the building of Indian history, these, and many more. Through those heartbreaking years of defeat and war, and back beyond, they gleam like priceless jewels in a diadem of many jewels. Why, then, are there today

[1] From *Black Elk Speaks*, by John G. Neihardt. Copyright, 1932, by the author. Used by permission of William Morrow & Co.

so few Indian leaders able to render their race distinguished service? Is the race no longer able to produce
great men? Why is Indian leadership frequently denied
a voice?

A PRIMARY REASON

Captivity cost the Indian his power to choose his own
leadership. In practically every realm of his life he has
had to accept leaders chosen for him by white men—
leadership in matters pertaining to his health, his education, his property, and, in most instances where he has
accepted Christianity, his religion, also. And this selection has been made according to the white man's cri-
teria, not the Indian's.

Reservation life destroyed the practical functions of
the old leaders. There was no longer room for movement of the people; no war, no hunting. And the Federal government, now holding the people in captivity,
made no effort to find new scope for their genius. On
the contrary, there occurred a period of suffocation of
Indian initiative carried on by a deliberate, planned destruction of whatever Indian leadership may have sur-
vived.

There grew up a feeling among the people that an
Indian accepting government favors or employment had
"sold out" the people. The Indian people frequently
refused to follow those Indians selected by the government for leadership, doubting their loyalty to the welfare of the people, but more particularly because the
individuals themselves did not have the inherent

strengths Indians demanded of their leaders. Too often the principal reason for their selection by the white official was submissiveness to white domination. So there grew up the fiction that Indians cannot be successfully employed for work in their own tribal group—a fiction that still influences Indian employment today.

This theory has surprisingly universal credence in spite of the past history of the race, and in spite of considerable evidence to the contrary in modern times. The Five Tribes in Oklahoma maintained their own tribal schools and other tribal institutions as long as they kept their tribal autonomy, and these were staffed almost entirely by tribal members. The Cherokee National Seminary, in operation as late as 1907, was so successful in its development of strong native leadership that even today its influence is vital in the tribe.

The church can point to examples that prove the fallacy of the theory that Indians are incapable of leadership of their own people, though the examples are all too few for the three hundred years that Christian churches have been committed to the program of training native leadership. Philip Deloria (Tipi Sapa) spent a long and fruitful life as an Episcopal clergyman, working in the very center of his own family circle, among his own Dakotas. Tipi Sapa was a great and strong man, and the qualities of leadership within himself enhanced the glory of his message to his people. His son, Vine Deloria, following in his father's footsteps, is also a Christian minister. He has recently been called to a church that serves both members of his own tribe and the white church members of the community where he is using his complete knowledge of Dakota life and Dakota ways and his racial identity with his own people to augment his own very real powers of leadership.

Oscar Gardner, who is now the president of the Oklahoma Regional Fellowship Conference of the National Fellowship of Indian Workers, is a Choctaw Indian who is working as a minister among members of the Choctaw tribe. Earl Riley, a Creek, is now president of Bacone College, which is attended by many Creek Indians and sponsored by many Creek alumni. Robert Chaat, himself a Comanche, is a pastor of the Comanche Reformed Church, to which he was called by the Comanche membership and which he has served with distinction for many years to the joy and benefit of his people. George Alvin Smith and Joseph Hanks, both Chippewas, were recently ordained to the priesthood of the Protestant Episcopal Church and are serving as missionaries to their own tribesmen. Albert Negahnquet was ordained a Roman Catholic priest in 1903 and returned to work among his own people. There are others, and as their numbers increase, so will the work of the church advance, and the hearts of the people be uplifted.

Wherever strong Indian leaders have been at work, a forward-looking program for all the people has developed and youth have been challenged to prepare for their own life work with hope and courage.

WHAT HAPPENED IN A PARTNERSHIP

It is no accident that the large majority of the Dakota Indians are active, participating Christians. Nor is this because the Dakota people have a greater propensity for the Christian faith than have many other tribes. There is doubtless more than one cause, but surely one is the willingness of the early leaders of Christianity among this tribe to take the Dakotas into partnership in the work of building a church among them.

Thomas S. Williamson, M.D., who has been called the "Father of Dakota Missions," went into the Dakota country in 1834 at the request of the American Board of Commissioners for Foreign Missions, to be followed three years later by the Reverend Stephen R. Riggs and his wife. These two men and their assistants laid the foundations and policies for the later mission work of the Presbyterian, Congregational, and Episcopal churches in the Dakotas. Simultaneously with their great tasks of reducing the Dakota language to writing, translating the Bible into the language of the people, compiling a Dakota dictionary, and translating text books into the Dakota tongue, these first missionaries began at once to train native workers to carry the gospel to other Indians.

The workers of the Protestant Episcopal Church, who came later, gave special emphasis to the development of Indian leadership. Wise beyond the expectation of the times, this great church, under the influence of

Bishop Hare, went to the Dakota people in the midst of their deepest suffering and offered to their rightful leaders a chance to guide their people into a new life. Bishop Hare, and his church behind him, had the courage and the vision to believe in the ability of the people. To carry the message of the church, he took men like Tipi Sapa, men already holding prestige within their group; men who knew the language and the customs of the people, and who were recognized by the people as strong and able men. Throughout his long ministry to the Sioux, Bishop Hare worked constantly to raise up a native ministry. While the government refused to hand over leadership to the Indians until the Indian could make himself understood in English, this church carried its message to the people in the native tongue and dared to give them full power in the direction of church activities. Today, therefore, the Protestant Episcopal Church is a powerful, living force in the lives of many Dakota people.

"The Indians love their church," writes Bishop Roberts. "They are very devout in their services, and they go farther to attend services and give more generously for the work of the church, in proportion to their means, than any other people I have ever known."

BLUEPRINT FOR TOMORROW

The hard journey of the Indian people through those years when the majority could have no voice in their civil affairs is approaching an end. For the spirit abroad in the world that cries out against the arbitrary domination of one people over another speaks for Indians, too. Already there is tangible evidence that this spirit is permeating all work with Indians, and from this point on the movement will be forward. For when Indians discover again their own powers of leadership, they will insist on the right to determine for themselves the disposition of matters that affect Indian communities. This self-determination has already begun to operate through several mediums.

One avenue through which Indian leadership is today making itself felt is the modern tribal council. Sometime during any month one may see a group of Indian men moving together about the halls of the central Office of Indian Affairs. There will be old men with long braids and dark, serious faces. Their shirts of bright color and vivid striped blankets add splendor to the aura of dignity about them. There will also be middle-aged men in the group, wearing hair cropped short and blue business suits more like modern America than the older Indian fashion. Usually, too, there is at least one younger man, smiling and friendly, who is along, one guesses, because he speaks English well and is skillful at interpreting. These are delegates from some tribal council who have come to do business for the tribe with their Federal government.

The tribal council is today the instrument of local government on Indian reservations through which the will of the people is expressed. It is an elective body directly responsible to the people for its performance in matters affecting tribal interest. The size of the council and the method of its election are determined by laws and regulations that the people themselves have adopted.

As these councils have developed, there has been a rebirth of Indian energy and Indian initiative. There has been a quickening into new life of Indian hope and self-confidence. In reading the minutes of the various tribal council meetings one senses the awakening of that same Indian spirit, adventurous and strong, that has held the people together through change and disaster and will lead them once again into a new life.

At first there is evident lack of confidence in themselves and in their own abilities.

"I don't know whether we can look at it at all or not at this time," one tribal leader speaks of the Re-organization Act that aimed to give back to the tribes the dignity and power of self-rule, "because in self-government we are very lacking in material, good material, and men as leaders."

"One thing that holds us back is lack of education," said another. "We need it, oh, in the worst way. We know it, and nobody knows it as we ourselves."

Then a growing self-confidence is revealed.

"In years gone by the government ran everything and all we did was sit back and kick. We said they were squandering our money if they built a dam or a ditch. Now we have control. Therefore, aren't we capable of solving this problem? Let us give it our best thought.

and come back tomorrow and voice our own ideas and opinions."

"Navajos are not strong enough yet to enter into the white man's industrial world—we may have to wait some time for that," declared a member of that large and vigorous tribe, "but right now we are able to enter into our own world and make a success of it if we stick together."

Then one discerns a sense of dignity and self-respect.

"If we cry for every little thing, then we are not men enough to get out of our cradles sooner," declared one council member.

And a tribal chairman said to the Indian Office officials, in concluding a conference, "We have not had much to say about relief. Relief is necessary. We know that you know it is, and that you are doing all you can. But now, and from now on, we are going to play down relief, not play it up. Through many previous years relief has come first and all subjects afterward when we have conferred at your office. It is not going to be that way in the future."

"It is a new thing," remarked another councilman, "to be treated as if we were grown men and given a voice in our own affairs, instead of being pushed around like automatons as we were in the past."

The tribal council members concern themselves with matters affecting the life of the tribe. They pass laws and ordinances governing tribal behavior; they determine the use of certain tribal assets; they advise with social workers on relief needs on the reservation; they handle credit funds for individual tribal members, and manage cooperative enterprises; they keep the people informed of changing Federal policies; and they assist in carrying out plans the Indian Office may wish to inaugurate.

Typical of the work of the tribal councils is the program of health education undertaken and carried out by the Rosebud Tribal Council of Rosebud Agency, South Dakota. As a first step in the health campaign this tribal council adopted a resolution calling attention to the prevalence of tuberculosis and trachoma and other infectious diseases, pointing out the benefit of examination and immediate hospitalization. Next the council appointed health committees of Indians residing in each community whose function it was to educate the people to isolate those who became ill and to encourage them to go at once for hospitalization. Two health meetings a year where health films were shown and health talks given were scheduled in each community. After a year of this kind of education the council next passed an ordinance imposing a fine on any person taking children into a home where there was active tuberculosis. This program for better health practices, the Indian Service officials say, has been more successful than anything done before because it has been carried out through leadership from within the group.

In similar ways Indians all over the United States are attacking whatever problems may confront them through the leadership of men they elect to serve on their tribal councils. These tribal councils are not, I am sure, the final word in Indian self-government. Indeed, even now, there are tribes who do not have such governing bodies. But the councils are one form of current self-government that Indians have to meet their needs of today. As those needs change, and as Indians grow in experience, it will be their right, as it has been the right of every community in our democracy, to change their methods of government if change will best serve their purpose. But whatever form Indian tribal government may take, one may legitimately hope these experiences in governing his own affairs will lead the Indian, as it has every other citizen of our country, into the larger responsibility of sharing fully in the government of the nation.

TRAINING FOR MODERN LEADERSHIP

These new responsibilities have called for a better trained Indian leadership, and, foreseeing this need, the Indian Re-organization Act increased the Federal educational loan fund to an amount adequate to meet the needs of Indian youth desiring advanced training in professions or trades but having no means of financing such education. This loan fund since its inception in 1931 has aided twenty-three hundred Indian students in many different types of training. The money is lent without interest to students whose records show promise of success and who are recommended by a committee from their local communities. The student selects his own school, but he is generally encouraged to go to the college or university nearest his home. This is because it is desirable for him to learn to know in college those men and women with whom he will later be associating professionally and because it is important for white neighbors to know the Indian student as well as the Indian relief client if they are to have a true understanding of the race among whom they have come to live.

What do these Indian boys and girls study when they borrow from the government loan fund? And what do they do with their training?

Phillip chose architecture. He came from a reservation in the far North where the people are very poor. He had no resources and no family who could help him, but he was determined to borrow as little as possible, so he worked for a large share of his college expenses. He graduated with honors, in the middle of the depression, and took a job at thirty dollars a month and maintenance. But he kept on giving his best until he is now well established in his profession with his total loan repaid.

Steven wanted forestry. He was not a brilliant student and he had to repeat some of his courses. But his determination and hard work carried him through to graduation. He was a forester with the National Park Service until he enlisted in the Navy.

Emily is an occupational therapist. She comes from one of the Pueblo villages of the Southwest where art is a natural vocation. Graduating with a degree in art from

her state university, she studied a year at an eastern
school of occupational therapy. She is working now at
her profession in a tuberculosis sanatorium of the Indian Service.

James was perhaps the most brilliant of all. He graduated from his state university, where he was made a
member of Phi Beta Kappa, and worked there for a
year on a fellowship while earning his master's degree.
He was later awarded a scholarship to complete his work
for the degree of doctor of philosophy at another university, but he, too, left school to join the armed forces.

Edith studied nursing and worked in the Indian Service three years. When war was declared, she enlisted as
a nurse in the Navy.

Sally completed her course in home economics at
the agricultural college of her state and returned to her
home reservation as a teacher of home economics for
the Indian Service.

Marian was interested in beauty culture, so she borrowed from the loan fund for this training. She completed the course and worked at her trade until she
was married.

And so the record goes through all the long list of
students. They have gone into schools all over the
United States for their specialized training. Some completed high school at government Indian schools; others
are graduates of public high schools in the towns and
cities of America. Many are graduates of mission schools;

in fact most of them have had, at some time or other during their elementary or high school days, some mission school experience. In their advanced courses in college or trade schools, some of the Indian students have been brilliant successes; some have failed and returned home; but like students everywhere the largest number have completed their courses with average success and those not in the armed forces, where most of the boys and many of the girls are today, are working at their vocations as average, dependable employees. The list of the vocations entered by these Indian students reads very much as such a list from any community of our country. The highest number have prepared for commercial work—stenography, accounting, bookkeeping. The next highest number have trained for teaching; then nursing; then agriculture, forestry, and engineering. One is a doctor with complete medical training and one a dentist. Two others are now in medical school. Among the trades the most popular are welding, beauty culture, baking, cooking, carpentry, electricity, and machine work.

"I believe this pays the government back in full money value for the money borrowed," writes a loan student from a Naval Air Station, "but I'm sure it can't pay back the value I received from its use. I don't think there is any other country in the world that would do for its people what has been done for me. That's why I'm doing my best to keep it that way."

INDIAN LEADERSHIP WITHIN THE INDIAN
SERVICE

A deep sense of responsibility to their own race is common among young Indians today, and many prefer to stay within the circle of their own racial group, if work opportunities permit them to choose.

"I want to learn how to help my people find a better way to live," is the reason frequently given by young Indians for wanting advanced training. Perhaps it is the deplorable economic condition of their parents and neighbors that brings this spirit of service to the group so widely into being; perhaps it grows out of the culture of a people who have since time immemorial put service to the group of first importance. Or it may be the influence of their mission school training that places an emphasis on service to others. Operating also, undoubtedly, are the idealism of youth and the natural desire of all human beings to remain with their kind. Whatever the reason may be, it is generally true that many Indian youth hope to return to the Indian country to work when their period of training is over.

Today the unnatural employment situation resulting from the war has taken many young Indians from their homes and families into the cities. Whether all will stay there after the war is over, or whether they will return to live among their own people, no one knows. Some, undoubtedly, will have made their adjustments to city life and will prefer to remain; some will not be able to adjust; and others from choice will probably return to the more simple rural life.

For those Indians who wish to return to the reservation the Indian Service, the church in its missionary program, and the public schools attended by large numbers of Indian children are the only avenues through which professionally trained Indians can find employment.

"One of the severest criticisms of the Indian Service and implicitly of Indians as well, in all the years gone by," writes Commissioner Collier, "has been the preponderance of whites employed in Indian Service of all types." [1]

After more than fifty years of an avowed policy of preferential employment of Indians, this preponderance of white employees still exists in the Indian Service and becomes more pronounced as the responsibility and salary of the position increases. In actual practice the policy of preferential employment of Indians for work in the Indian Service has meant preference mainly for those jobs with less responsibility and pay. The last survey made of the number of Indians working in the Indian Service revealed that more than two-thirds of the total number employed were in the lowest salary brackets, while only one per cent were in positions responsible enough to insure some participation in its policy-working functions. This means that in the main Indian employees have far too little opportunity to help in the

[1] *Indians at Work*, October, 1933.

determination of administrative policies, for they are largely working in jobs under the supervision of some white employees, jobs which, because of their routine character, rarely offer opportunity for courageous initiative. As a result, many able Indians, discouraged at the apparent handicaps for advancement, are going into work unrelated to that of the Indian Service and often far away from Indian country. Thus, much of the best material for leadership is lost to the Indian people.

There are several reasons why Indian ability is not more generally recognized and used. Three stand out, and each influences the others. There is among many white employees of the Indian Service, and much of the general public as well, a firm belief that Indians are irresponsible, "just like children," and incapable of being trusted with serious responsibility. It is difficult for such people to believe any Indian could carry a responsible job. The second reason is perhaps more subtle and often entirely unconscious. A growing Indian leadership threatens vested interests. The boss, who likes his pleasant job and who does not wish to relinquish it, finds it easy to believe the Indian "is not ready yet" for any kind of responsibility that might lead eventually into his own domain. The third reason is the failure of the Indian Office to carry through any organized plan of discovering and grooming successful Indian employees for the more responsible jobs that will eventually open.

Three times the Congress of the United States has appropriated modest funds for the initiation of an in-service training program that would insure Indians a larger share in the direction of their own Indian Service. Each time the Commissioner of Indian Affairs and his policy-making staff in all good faith conceived and put into operation such a program. But each time the enterprise has "bogged down" in details and competing demands that it would seem a more determined zeal might have overcome. The salaries in these so-called in-service training jobs have been kept at an extremely low level on the theory that the Indian employee was receiving training on the job that would compensate for lack of salary and lead eventually to promotion to a better job. But since neither training nor promotion often materialized it would appear to the unprejudiced observer that at least the first two attempts at in-service training for Indians have largely deteriorated into a scheme for cheap labor on a racial basis. The third and most recent attempt is still being worked out.

One in-service training project that was successful until the war forced its discontinuance should be mentioned. Several teaching apprenticeships were established whereby young Indian college graduates prepared for teaching were trained under Indian Service teachers considered to be unusually successful. Both the work of the apprentice and the teacher was carefully supervised and promotions consistently carried through. More than fifty young Indian teachers came into the Indian Service in this manner with excellent advantage to themselves and to the Service.

LEADERSHIP IN THE INDIAN CHURCHES

The record of the churches in the use and training of Indian leadership is little better than that of the Federal government. As pointed out earlier, after more than three hundred years of effort, trained Indian leaders in the church are conspicuous by their fewness. While there are on some reservations well trained Indian missionaries, the majority of Indian workers employed in the missionary activities of most of the churches are in the lower paid positions. Although there is an up-swing here also, and conditions are slowly changing, any conference on Indian missionary policies and methods is still usually overwhelmingly white in its make-up. The reasons behind this situation are much the same as those behind the Federal government's handling of the same problem. The churches have long recognized the need and advantages of native leadership. But it has not seen clearly enough that Indian youth, as the youth of any people, are challenged by opportunity; by examples of successful achievement; and by live, active programs that meet their need and the needs of their communities. If the program of the church is to be effective in the lives of the people, it is the competent, ambitious, able youth who must be challenged into its leadership.

As long as so many of the Indian workers of the mission field are ill-equipped, poorly paid, and hold uncertain status, many capable Indians will be discouraged from entering mission work. Moreover, white workers will drift into the habit of believing the present leadership the best of which the race is capable because it is the only leadership they know. It is encouraging to see that many churches are working on a program to secure better trained Indian leadership, both in the ordained ministry and among the lay workers.

INTERDENOMINATIONAL LEADERSHIP

Most of the denominational differences found in America have their origin in a history totally foreign to Indians. The rivalry between the denominations at work on some mission fields has frequently hindered rather than advanced the cause of Christianity among Indians. They have frequently been unable to understand these differences or to see why so much weight and importance should be given to them, since in the end all lead to the same God, and all teach of the same Christian love.

One of the most effective programs of leadership training is the work being carried on by religious work directors in several of the government Indian schools through the cooperative efforts of fifteen different denominational boards. Students who come to the government non-reservation boarding schools are from many different sections of the country and from many different mission fields where they have been nurtured under a particular denominational banner. The interdenominational approach is the only effective means of reaching these students. The entire program of the religious work directors in the government schools is pointed toward giving students experiences and techniques in Christian leadership that will enable them to be more effective in their church and community affairs on return to their homes.

At Haskell Institute, where Russell Carter has been religious work director for more than eight years, all the group meetings are student-led, and students help in the planning of all activities. "There are two objectives for my work here," says this director: "to break down the barrier between religion and life—make the students understand that religion is life; and to teach the students how to become active members in their church organizations wherever they may be." In line with these objectives, there is a student discussion group managed by the students where the problems they must meet as they go into the cities or back home are faced frankly and without squeamishness in brisk, lively discussion.

The church school program at Haskell is in the hands of students, with all student officers, the religious director remaining in the background to give counsel when asked, but holding frequent meetings with the student leaders to give direction where it is needed. There are numerous requests from neighboring communities for the student teams who go out frequently to conduct services. In this manner students get valuable experience in conducting community meetings, experience doubly important now that Indians are assuming greater control over their community affairs through implementation of the Indian Re-organization Act.

At Flandreau School students frequently assume full charge of services at the local church when there is no resident pastor, and here also student groups conduct services at other schools and community churches under the guidance of the religious work director.

The Young Women's Christian Association in Indian schools has long been a pioneer in this field. This organization, together with the Young Men's Christian Association, first led Indian students into wider acquaintance with the outside world. The student conferences at which Indian students shared experiences with white students gave many of us our first idea that other people beside ourselves had problems, too, and of how these problems were solved by them. The Indian Y.W.C.A. at Carlisle Indian School was sending delegates to the Northfield, Massachusetts, Y.W.C.A. conferences as early as 1896.

FROM SCHOOL TO LOCAL CHURCH

In the local churches on the reservations, a greater effort is being made to stimulate the Indian membership to assume more responsibility for their own church program. One Indian pastor who was trained at Bacone College and Eastern Baptist Theological Seminary holds classes once a week to instruct the lay workers in his church how to teach a Sunday school class and how to lead a devotional service; and he and the groups discuss how they, working together, can make the church a better, stronger institution.

"In the old days," says this young Indian minister, "the missionaries did everything for the Indian people. I am trying to get the Indian people to do everything for themselves."

He is carrying this objective into all the realms of church activity, even to keeping up the building and grounds. His community is too poor to employ a church janitor, so the members of the church take turns keeping the church premises in good order.

There is a growing body of young Indians at work on the mission fields who received their inspiration and training at Bacone College. This Christian junior college has enriched the lives of Indian students from all over the United States. Through its doors have passed Indian youth who have become teachers, lawyers, ministers, farmers; they are strong Christian leaders wherever they have gone. Many were helped by the college to secure scholarships for more advanced training that has made possible fruitful careers. Bacone College emphasizes Christian leadership in its whole curriculum, but there are special courses in leadership training, in Bible study, and in community recreation. Students are given actual practice in group discussion, in leading group meetings, in teaching Sunday school classes and conducting church services. Once each month students from the college go out to near-by Indian churches to lead the church service for that Sunday.

The Cook Christian Training School at Phoenix, Arizona, formerly operated by the Presbyterian Church in the United States of America, is now an interdenominational institution operating under the Home Missions Council for the purpose of training Indian ministers and lay church members in the work of the church. "It seeks to give these workers practical skills and knowledge of most effective methods and material for their use, and to deepen their personal Christian life," explains the director of the school.

To this school come husbands and wives, seeking new vision and better ways of doing old tasks. The wives study homemaking and club work in order to be better helpmates to their minister husbands. The children attend special services at Cook School but are sent to the public schools of Phoenix for their regular school work. The husbands study English, Bible, and public speaking and get practical experience in near-by Indian churches, in visiting the sick, and in teaching Bible courses at the Phoenix school.

One of the functions of Cook School is to direct those who are especially gifted to the excellent junior college near by or to the State Teachers College for more thorough academic preparation. The school is keenly alert to the need of preparing a native ministry to serve better a completely rural people, and its program is shaped around rural needs.

A very real test of the influence of mission schools is the part graduates take in church and community life when they return to the reservation or go to live in some town or city after completing their school work.

THE MINISTRY OF HEALING

Healing has always been the business of the church. At Ganado, Arizona, in the very heart of the Navajo desert, there is an oasis in the form of the Presbyterian mission. Here an excellent hospital is serving the Navajo people, and connected with it is a school of nursing to which Indian girls from all the Indian country, even from Alaska, come for training. Many return to their home communities to work as nurses in the Indian Service or in some mission station. Many have lately gone into the armed forces to work beside their white sister-nurses in the service of their country. Wherever these Indian nurses go, they too may be thought of as leaders of their people.

WHY AN INDIAN LEADERSHIP?

There are many reasons why there must be vigorous Indian leadership if the race is to grow. Indian young people need the inspiration of competent Indian leadership against which to measure their own potentialities. From some source confidence in one's self must be fed. Though the ancient springs are deep and clear, Indian youth cannot always look backward. They must see about them modern leaders of their own era and their own race if they are to achieve any sense of security in the new life they must enter. Some years ago an Indian was placed at the head of one of the largest, best-known government Indian schools. It was the first time a full-blood Indian had been given such recognition. Students on his campus and Indian students all over the United States walked straighter, worked more joyously, because he was there. His achievement freed their wills to reach toward undreamed-of stars.

"He was born in a tepee," one of the boys who wanted to be a doctor told me with glowing face. "And he lived just like my folks, not even speaking English until he was almost as old as I am now. If he can get two degrees from Yale University and be superintendent of this school, I know I can be a doctor!"

And across the continent an old Indian man whose long braids were thin with age and frosty white spoke to me through an interpreter.

"I am glad there is an Indian at the head of that school. That shows the Indians that anything a white man can do they can do also. Our young people need to know that sometimes."

The story is told that when Robert Chaat was seven years old he overheard his father and other deacons of the church praying the Lord to raise up a leader from among the Comanches to be pastor of their church. As he played his careless way through boyhood he pondered this memory in his heart, just as his youthful ancestors must have pondered the vision that came to guide them in the old days of long ago. And the memory became blended in the heart of the lad Robert with the story told him of his christening when the missionary had taken him in his arms and prayed God that he should grow up to be a leader of the Comanches, and with the memory of his parents who were the first among the Comanches to be converted to Christianity. He grew up, went away to school, and was married. He started out to be a farmer. But the pull of the memories was strong. And in 1934 he was ordained to the ministry of the Reformed Church in America, and called to be the pastor of the church of his people. Thus were fulfilled the prayers of the Comanches that a leader from among themselves might be sent to the people.

Only Indian leadership with undertsanding and deep appreciation of their racial past can awaken again in the hearts of the people that pride of race that once built a cultural tradition so strong, so beautiful, and can build it again. Only Indian leadership can bring to richest flowering that which is Indian in the life of the people.

It has been the history of all people that alien ways are accepted slowly and with reluctance. The experience of other nations with subject people has demonstrated that progress comes more rapidly if alien ways are introduced through native leadership. In Rhodesia, for example, the British made no headway in introducing modern scientific agriculture through white extension agents. Only when native workers were trained and returned to their home communities to farm and teach did the people listen and follow. America might with profit follow Rhodesia's example. Indian leadership has not yet had a chance to show what it can do.

6: THE OUTLOOK FOR THE FUTURE

> As my eyes search the prairie
> I feel the summer in the spring.
> —Chippewa [1]

THE commencement exercises at the Kiowa and Comanche school were over and the Director of Education for the Indian Service, who had just awarded the diplomas to the high school seniors, lingered on the steps of the auditorium to visit with a group of Indian parents. As one of the boy graduates passed out of the building, he caught the eye of his grandfather, who was standing in the center of the group, and flashed him a grin of triumph. With an almost imperceptible flick of the wrist, he waved at his grandfather the slim white scroll that he carried, the diploma that represented to them both so much effort and achievement. The old man's face remained impassive, for he was listening to the official from Washington. But in every angle of his gaunt old frame, wrapped so majestically in his scarlet blanket and his eighty winters, there was the stamp of pride.

[1] *Chippewa Indian Music II*, by Frances Densmore, p. 253. Used by permission of the Bureau of American Ethnology, Smithsonian Institution.

Soon afterward he spoke. "Indians make progress."

"How do you mean?" asked the Director of Education, who had missed none of the byplay between the old man and his grandson.

"Me—I am an old man," the grandfather answered in the broken accents of a language infrequently used. "I did not go to the white schools. I did not even learn to read English. My son there"—and he pointed to a middle-aged man walking with his family across the campus —"went to school only as far as the sixth grade. Today my grandson graduated from high school. His son, maybe, who is not yet born, will graduate from college a long time after I am no longer living. That is how Indians make progress."

That is how it must be. I saw clearly the meaning of this answer as I reviewed mentally the slow procession of the years moving across the pathway of a race, bringing with them change and new knowledge and a different kind of wisdom. In imagination I had a vision of young Indian boys and girls moving forward all down the centuries, each generation in its turn moving into a new and changing life. These latest generations, represented by the old man and his grandson, were experiencing the greatest and most inevitable changes of them all.

Thinkers among the Indian people have understood the inevitability of these changes in Indian life and have done what they could to help prepare their young people to meet them. "I know that my race must change,"

Chief Joseph said many years ago. "We cannot hold our own with the white man as we are. We can only ask an even chance to live as other men live. We ask to be recognized as men."

PROGRESS WILL COME THROUGH EDUCATION

There is no magic formula by which the dislocations in Indian life, caused by changes too drastic and too rapid, can be healed. It is only through the slow process of education that the best adjustments can be brought about. This must be an education carried to the people not only by the schools but by every activity that touches the individual Indian—the Indian home, the community, and the church as well as the classroom. The well-being of every facet of Indian life—health, employment, morality, law and order, the conservation of the very soil on which Indians walk and build their homes—is dependent on sound education in the common everyday skills that make for good American living. Writes one student of Indian affairs:

The Indian problem is largely one of race conservation and advancement. This means, in the large, education including not merely a common school or vocational training for children, but a process by which young and old, individual and family, community and nation, shall be taught to live and prosper in the increasingly complex society into which the rapidly turning wheels of fate have brought the Indian people. There is danger that good people, incensed by the wrongs that have been done the Indians, will, by stridently demanding that they be given their "rights," ignore the educational task before the American people in preserving and advancing the Indian race.[1]

It is through education, in all of its broad ramifications, that the white man has his easiest and most effective means of sharing with the Indian people the American way of life. But if there is to be a genuine sharing, as opposed to imposition, the Indian people must be permitted to have a voice in the kind of education provided for themselves and their children. Educational goals for Indians advanced by the white man have often not been Indian goals. At a conference of government school officials and Navajo parents that I once attended a group of Navajo men, speaking through an interpreter, made this very clear.

"Our children are ruined for the life they have to live here when they return from your schools," they told the government officials. "They are no longer happy to spend long hours on the desert with the flocks. They have no peace. You have not put the desert and the sheep into their hearts as we would have done." The Navajo men were justly charging that the government schools had failed to develop in the Navajo child that love and respect for rural life that is essential if he is to know peace and harmony in the only kind of life often left open to him.

The Indian people themselves must be allowed—indeed, they must be obligated—to think through their

[1] Ray A. Brown, *Yale Law Journal*, January, 1930, Vol. 39, No. 3. Used by permission.

own problems and work out for themselves the kind of life they want. It is the task of the educator to stimulate this kind of decision through every technique at his command—conferences with the people, study clubs, discussion groups, programs, plays, demonstrations, Indian crafts, music, and art. Until Indians can begin in genuine earnest to attack their own problems, little that a benevolent government can do in the way of leading them back to self-reliance and economic competence will be effective.

WILL THE CHURCH AGAIN PIONEER?

What place has the church in such an educational program? In Indian history the church has always been the pioneer, moving ahead, trying out new methods, discovering new needs, and pointing the way for other agencies that came later. Will the church again point the way?

Since Indian youth are now staying at home to attend high school, and since many are settling down to live in permanent residences in the same area after school days are over, a program that will make rural life satisfying and challenging is demanded. The church in its mission work can supply such a program. In some places activities with this objective in view are already being undertaken. In one church in Nevada, for example, there is a men's club that meets twice each month. There is a Boy Scout troop, a sewing club for mothers, a music club for girls. At Dulce, New Mexico, where the Jicarilla Apaches live, there is a community house, maintained by the Reformed Church in America, that the Apaches are free to use at any time. There is a library, used constantly by some of the younger group who are most versatile in English. And in the laundry or the sewing room or at the bathhouse, Apaches of all ages may be found at most any hour of the day.

"If the church is to be strong in the lives of the young people," a veteran missionary to Indians said with the conviction of long years of experience, "we have to go into their home country and build up a practical, live community program."

The government schools are teaching youth how to make a living, but it is the church that must teach them how to live courageously and wisely, motivated and directed by spiritual power. Indian youth, like other youth, cannot find within themselves alone the strength or the vision to solve the intolerable difficulties that confront them. If they are to stand firm against all the forces that beat against them, they must have power greater than themselves and outside themselves. Only religion can provide the ideals and guides to right living so urgently needed. If the Christian church is to meet the challenge of Indian need, it has before it three primary tasks: to help Indians discover the inner power and control that only a deep religious conviction can give; to help Indians achieve a more abundant life economically, socially, spiritually; and to lead the white world into a more general acceptance of Indians as individuals.

WHAT LIES AHEAD?

No one so far has been able to make an assuring prediction of the future of the Indian people. We just do not know. There are some students of Indian affairs who believe that each step into the future leads all Indians farther along that broad highway toward complete identification with white American life. Such leaders point to places like Oklahoma, where the Cherokees, the Creeks, the Choctaws, the Delawares, and other tribes have, in general, merged well into the life of the state and are daily leaving the old Indian life farther behind. These friends of the Indian believe that the best service we can render him is to hasten in every possible way this process of assimilation.

There is another group, also very familiar with the Indian scene and eager to offer friendly assistance, who feel that assimilation is proceeding much more slowly than we may have supposed. They point to such groups as the Hopi (and there are many Indian groups much like the Hopi in greater or less degree) who stand today essentially unchanged after centuries of onslaught from an aggressive civilization that has pounded with the fury of a tornado against the doors of the tribal spirit. This group feels that to try to hasten the process of assimilation by outside pressure will have further devastating results; that social disintegration and death occurs when the valid elements of Indian culture are destroyed too rapidly, before equally valid elements of white culture can be substituted. They believe that, while it is probable that in the dim future all races and all civilizations may eventually blend into one people, each racial group, even the Indians, has the right to make that merging at its own pace and in its own individual way.

What place the Indian of the future will have in American life, we can only speculate. There are tribes whose economic foothold is so precarious that sheer survival is still uncertain. The matter of getting a bare subsistence is urgent and impelling. Today these groups, for reasons beyond their own power to remedy, are less nearly self-supporting than they were fifty years ago. The reservation lands, their home base, have shrunk so that they no longer can support many of the tribes. Some other means beside the land will have to be found to provide a living for a large majority of the growing Indian population.

And even now in many parts of America, the Indian is not accepted as an equal when he leaves his reservation in search of a livelihood. Racial prejudice operates strongly against him. There are localities where he cannot go into a restaurant to eat food when he is hungry; where he cannot get a room in a hotel when he is tired; where he is not welcome in the church, if his soul is weary or afraid. There are places where an Indian cannot rent a home in a decent neighborhood; where he cannot choose the kind of associates he would like for his children; and where he cannot secure the job that he is trained to do. As long as these conditions prevail how can we know what kind of tomorrow will dawn for the Indian?

DISCOVERIES THAT BRING HOPE

But there are some things that we have discovered that point toward a future of some promise. We now know that the Indian people are too strong to die. They are not vanishing, but are increasing in numbers and increasing rapidly. While there is much intermarriage and while many mixed-bloods are a part of the Indian population, we know that we have to deal with a hardy, vigorous people who will be with us as a racial group for a long time.

We know, too, that there are Indians who will die before they will leave their racial groups; that even economic necessity cannot drive some from the land of their fathers. And we know this group includes young Indians as well as old. For these the only hope of economic independence is to learn how to make maximum use of the resources of their reservation, the resources of human intelligence as well as of land.

But we also know that among Indians as among all other people, there are and there will continue to be many adventurous souls who will want to leave the home base, facing all obstacles in order to build a new life for themselves in a different environment. These will leave the reservations to plunge into the full current of American life. This is their right, and for these, as well as for those who stay at home, we are obligated to provide the kind of education that will prepare them for the life they want to live.

One other thing we have also learned. We now know that Indians and whites can work together. As late as 1938 I attended a conference of Indian Service officials at which one whole session was given over to a discussion of whether Indians would work as the white man works, if they had the chance. To me the tragedy in that discussion was not alone that so little understanding of human motivation and incentives was disclosed, but also that up until this late date in Indian-white relationships, Indians as a group had not had a convincing opportunity to prove that they could and would work!

The records of Indians who are now being employed daily in industry, the ordnance depots, the railroad shops, and on the ranches and farms all over America give definite evidence that Indians are proficient workers in jobs they understand and that they can work in friendliness with the white men who labor beside them. As the two races come to know each other better through working together, the amity between them grows and misunderstandings and discriminations decrease.

In the summer of 1943 I attended the Oklahoma regional conference of the National Fellowship of Indian Workers. This organization, sponsored by the Home Missions Council, was formed "to establish and to foster a unity of spirit and service among Indian missionaries, mission board members, government employees, and other friends of the Indian, to affirm their group consciousness, to share their experiences, and to establish orderly means to discuss any matters affecting the welfare of Indians and Indian missions."

At the Oklahoma meeting there were Indian delegates and white delegates. What interested me and impressed me deeply was that except for pigmentation there was absolutely no difference apparent between the white delegates and the Indian delegates. There were no identifying differences in points of view or in methods of approach or in attitudes. If I had not known from old acquaintance which delegates were Indian and which white, it would have been difficult to tell. Even color of skin was not always a distinguishing characteristic. There was a tall, dignified judge present who I was sure was white but who turned out to be an Indian. And there was a dark-complexioned missionary who I was certain was an Indian but who, I learned later, was white.

Among the members of the two races, there was complete understanding and mutual respect. An Indian was president of the conference and he was enthusiastically re-elected to continue in office for the next conference. Three days were spent in a discussion of Indian problems, but these problems were approached as human problems caused by sociological conditions that might have manifested themselves in exactly the same ways in any group of people. The conference became three days of brotherhood and fellowship and another demonstration that Indians and whites can work out their problems together.

In the long struggle to help Indians live in harmony and peace in America, many blunders have been made by both races. As our horizons have widened, our vision has become clearer and slowly, inch by inch, step by step, there has been progress. We are still far from perfection. There are still shortcomings to be remedied, injustices to be righted. But the movement is still forward. Our insight has deepened, and in many ways America is farther along the road toward according justice to the Indian people. There are many examples of progress, but we have here space to cite only two of the more conspicuous.

Those of the dominant group no longer say to Indians who cling to the old ways, as in effect they once did, "Your differences from us are shameful. The sooner you put them aside and become like us the better it will be for you and the easier it will be for us to tolerate you."

Today they are saying instead, "We are beginning to doubt that your differences are even regrettable. It is entirely possible that they might be an asset both to you and to American life. They might add color and richness and variety. Anyhow you have a right to be different if that is what you want."

Such signs of changes in thinking promise that the time will come when all white Americans will be able to say:

"We need your differences, and those of other people who have come to live among us, to make all our lives richer and more complete. We need the contributions you can make to the composite life of America because of those differences."

The second conspicuous advance that has been made in thinking on Indian problems is that there is a growing tendency to recognize and use Indian ability. More Indian groups are doing things for themselves than ever before, and doing them successfully. As they acquire through such experience more and more realistic training in self-government, Indians will become increasingly unwilling to remain underprivileged and dominated social groups outside the body politic of the states in which they live. While full participation in American life has not been achieved, advancement is being made.

SELF-HELP THE INDIAN WAY

Indians, perhaps, understand the non-economic values of cooperative endeavor more clearly than do the white people of America, for that is the ancient Indian way. Now they are learning through organized cooperatives that there is economic advantage in communal effort. It is through these cooperatives that some of the most successful attacks on the Indians' economic problems are being made. There are increasing examples of successful enterprises run by Indians themselves.

The Jicarilla Apaches, many people thought, were too primitive and too backward to govern themselves. Twenty-six years ago they were a dying tribe, steeped in pessimism. Infant mortality was extreme and the death rate for all ages was high. The old men, out of some

deeply planted racial wisdom, found courage to face a
future of hopelessness and despair. It was the young who
opened listless fingers to let life slip silently into the
darkness of eternity. Moved four times by the Federal
government, these discouraged people were finally settled in the mountain region of New Mexico that is now
their home. But for two generations the Jicarilla Apaches
were denied the opportunity to work to support themselves. Their lands were leased for them to white cattle-
men for an amount that yielded each individual only
about twenty dollars a year. Privation, disease, drunken-
ness, idleness, and despair were the lot of all the tribe.
Seventy-five per cent were thought to be infected with
tuberculosis. Into this hopeless situation there came a
new superintendent who believed in the capacities of
the Jicarilla people and understood their desperate need.
With tribal funds from the sale of Jicarilla timber he
purchased sheep and the Apaches went to work. Over a
continuing period of twenty-five years, the policies he set
in motion have been carried out.

When opportunity came for the Jicarillas to organize
under the Indian Re-organization Act, the tribe voted
unanimously for self-government. Their constitution was
adopted by a vote of two hundred and forty-two to two.
Today the Jicarillas are increasing in numbers and they
are to the forefront among the independent, progressive
Indian tribes.

At Neilsville, Wisconsin, the Winnebago Indians are
operating a cooperative, sponsored by a missionary of

the Evangelical and Reformed Church, that is bringing
returns to its members in fellowship and mutual sharing
as well as in money values. Out of very simple begin-
nings this cooperative has become an effective movement for economic self-help. Its purpose is to produce
and to find a market for the beautiful Winnebago baskets, beadwork, and other handicrafts.

Indian young people, too, are learning to do things in
a genuinely cooperative way. To the Albuquerque Indian School one day there came four visitors from
Mexico who told the student body of their Indian
cousins south of the border. The senior class decided
they would like to visit Mexico and learn something of
the customs of Indians there and to tell those Mexican
Indians something of their own traditions and ways of
living, "so we can better understand one another," as
the class president explained. "You can go," the class
adviser told the group, "if you will earn the money to
pay for the trip."

The class set to work. They built a school canteen,
sold hamburgers, candy, and pop. They gave programs
of Indian dances and legends in Albuquerque and neighboring towns. They held nickelodeon dance programs at
the school. The boys worked at any jobs they could get
and pooled their wages. The two thousand dollars necessary to pay for the trip slowly accumulated. In the mean-
time the students kept careful accounts and learned
about costs and travel requirements. They made arrange-
ments with the Department of Education in Mexico

about the schools and villages they were to visit and the important things to see. At last, immediately after graduation, the class of seventy-two students set out on the trip for which they had planned and worked so faithfully. From the point of view of the students the trip was highly successful. "By exchanging ideas with the Mexican students," they said later, "we gained a better understanding of one another and a closer feeling of friendship."

Indians are also attempting to solve other problems besides the basic one of economic security. There are many thousands of Indians of mixed blood who are, culturally speaking, white men. Shall they continue indefinitely to be legal Indians? Treaty obligations, allotted lands, and the human desire to share in tribal equities have made it difficult to secure legislation to terminate their Indian status. The Blackfeet in Montana and other tribes are working on this problem and attempting to solve it by limiting tribal participation to a minimum degree of Indian blood.

What of law and order on Indian reservations? Shall Indians continue indefinitely to live under a different legal system as long as they remain within the boundaries of a reservation? Some tribes do not think so and are considering asking for legislation to place their reservations under the jurisdiction of state and county laws. As education becomes more general and white culture more diffused among the Indian people, this doubtless will be the desire of many Indian tribes.

Shall Indian lands continue to be untaxed? Indian groups are becoming increasingly aware that special exemptions of this nature create against them prejudice and ill will. They know that even though they pay all taxes except the tax on property, exempted by treaty agreement or by an act of Congress, the fact of this one omission stands out in people's minds to their disadvantage. Indians are coming to understand that if they are to share fully in all the privileges of citizenship, they must carry all its obligations.

These are only a few of the myriad problems affecting their lives that Indians are at last attempting to solve for themselves through group thinking and group action.

FRIENDS CAN HELP

How can all Americans who believe in freedom and justice and good will help Indian Americans to help themselves? Are there ways by which Christians can express the friendship they feel toward those of Indian heritage in their midst? What can be done to solve the vexing problems that in one way or another affect the life of every Indian?

You can begin by treating all Indians whom you meet as human beings like yourselves, giving them the same chance to prove themselves that you would give one of your own group. If Tom is slow, you can say, "That is just like Tom," instead of the words heard more frequently, "Oh, well, that is just like an Indian." When Indians come to your church services or community programs, you can make them feel at home rather than allowing them to sit, as I have often seen them, in a corner by themselves, a diffident, lonely little group. Simple things to do, these two suggestions, but they are fundamental to a satisfactory solution of the whole Indian problem.

"But," there are those who will say, "I never meet an Indian where I live, and none come to my church. How can I help?" Every time you insist that the privileges of democracy be given to members of any minority group, whenever you stress their right to be a minority with differences that are respected, you help to create a climate of freedom and good will from which Indians will also profit. These benefits will overflow to the betterment of Indian life just as truly as the economic prosperity created throughout the United States by the war lifted some of the shadows of poverty from Indian homes.

There are many other opportunities ahead of all of us. We can, if we will, face the past, use it to understand the present, and then move forward. Nothing is to be gained by dwelling morbidly on yesterday's sorrows. Memories of the old griefs, old wrongs, and old animosities have too often stood in the way of progress. Indians need to be helped by the attitudes of their friends to move away from the past toward a more promising future.

You can, if you will, measure all that you do by this yardstick: *What really counts is the kind of person your efforts tend to produce.* You can acknowledge with gratitude all that is good in Indian tradition. You can accept your responsibility for the types of laws and kind of administration that govern so large a part of Indian life. This means that you will need to keep yourselves informed about legislation affecting Indians and that you will need to be intelligent about the issues that are advocated for their benefit.

Legislation advocated for the Indians is sometimes instigated by the selfish interests of those who want Indian possessions or initiated by individuals friendly enough but too shortsighted to look ahead to the consequences. It is your obligation to give thoughtful study to the issues that vitally affect the well-being of these people who are so dependent on the actions of Congress.

Many of these issues are extremely complex. The matter of wardship is one typical example. You will doubtless hear some thoughtless person declare, "Wardship is bad. It ought to be abolished at once." On the face of it, you may be tempted to agree to hasty action before you realize the tragic catastrophe such sudden removal of protection would bring to many Indians. There is need for careful study before a satisfactory method can be worked out for those who still need helpful supervision in managing their property. So with many other problems that the voters of this country, through their Congress, have to settle for Indians. As long as large numbers of Indians are disenfranchised, your responsibility to them is doubly heavy.

If you accept the responsibility of helping the Indian to find ways out of his difficulties, it will lead you to struggle with the economic problems that enmesh Indian lives. You will be forced to seek some means of securing a more abundant physical life for them. It will involve you in the process of securing political democracy for all Indians. It will mean sending into the Indian Service the kind of employee who believes in the democratic way of life and who is, therefore, unwilling to exercise uncontrolled authority over the lives of another people.

You can, if you will, put yourselves squarely against segregation for all people. There are two kinds of segregation that Indians face.

There is first the geographical segregation caused by the early Federal policy of isolation that created the reservations. This cannot now be remedied, for surely no government would again uproot a people who are finding ways to begin once more the rhythm of their life. America can, of course, see to it that Indians are free to choose whether they are to live on the reservation or in some white community. Free choice, of necessity, also involves decision regarding the kind of education that will equip Indians for life either off or on the reservation.

But the second kind of segregation that no Indian chooses to face is that caused by racial prejudice. There are public schools where Indian children are not accepted. There are localities where Indians cannot compete as wage earners. There are places where white men feel that it is fair to cheat and exploit an Indian.

"We would like to dress as white girls do," said a group of Navajo girls whom I know, "but the only places we can wear those clothes after we leave school are the streets of Gallup and the low joints around the town. We are not welcome in the better places."

The Christian church, because it stands for the brotherhood of all mankind, can, more than any other agency, help to pave the way for Indian acceptance in the white world. There is an opportunity for a far more vigorous program in this field.

The church can insist that Indian leadership be used in our church and government programs. This is a very important way to encourage Indian youth to seek further training and make the most of their abilities.

One obstacle to the advancement of Indian leadership has been the lack of professional training. This has not been due to lack of ability but to the high cost of postgraduate study and to the dearth of scholarships and fellowships available for Indians. Most positions of responsibility in the educational field call for training beyond the college level. The majority of Indians who complete college courses have to borrow for this purpose and their debts are too great to leave them free for the advanced professional study that is essential. This is the chief reason why there are so few Indian physicians. The church can help Indian youth greatly by providing more scholarships and fellowships for them.

COME AND MEET MY FRIEND

A woman whom I visited recently is, it seems to me, a symbol of the Indian of today and tomorrow. She comes from a tribe that the average American would call "backward"—a people who still live in the ancient manner high in the mountains that have been their home for time upon time. Her family stayed in the hills, but she went to a mission school and there married a man from another tribe. Now both of them are employed by the mission school and it is the home that they have created there on that campus that I visited.

Everywhere about the lovely pine-paneled house there were signs of competence and skill—outward evidence of a normal, happy integration of white and Indian culture. My hostess, a full-blood Indian mother, was thoroughly at home in white ways of doing things and deft at white etiquette. Her quiet poise and assurance were reflected in her children. The dinner was typically white American—Southern fried chicken and Waldorf salad and all the other fixings—and very delicious. The shamrock stamped in the corner of the snowy white linen table-cloth was evidence that it had come from Ireland. On the bed there was a spread with an early colonial design that this woman had woven herself in the school craft shop. Yet all through the house there were signs of Indian things and Indian ways close and dear to all. On the walls were colorful Indian paintings and beaded wall hangings in Apache design, the latter the mother's handiwork. The doll the nine-year-old daughter displayed so proudly was also made by her mother, a perfect replica of a Dakota warrior in beaded buckskin and feathered war bonnet.

We talked of many things that summer evening, the mother and I. And through all the talk, like a golden thread winding in and out, ran the proud, warm memories of her Indian girlhood.

I remember clearly one thing she said. "They asked me to teach tanning here at the school. But I don't feel that I ought to do that because I never had the tanning ceremony. Among my people they give a ceremony for these skills to each member of the family. Of course, I know how to tan, but they gave the tanning ceremony to my sister. To me they gave the beadwork ceremony. That is why I am able to do beadwork so well." It was said quietly and without boasting, and somehow you knew the deeper meaning and the searching power that an ancient Indian ceremony, symbolical of an attitude of mind, had added to the simple skill of beadwork.

Through such glowing prisms one caught glimpses of her Indian heritage that had given treasures she would always possess. They were at the heart of a home that nourished well the seeds of other cultures planted there, a home where beauty and peaceful harmony were everywhere manifest.

Here is a woman in whose person is living evidence that the merging of Indian and white cultures need not be a destructive process. Under the right kind of circumstances this blending can build for the individual a more satisfying life and for the world a richer personality than any one culture could produce.

FOR INDIANS ARE PEOPLE, TOO

"This Indian problem, if there is one, is really so simple," said an employee of the Indian Service who had worked with Indians for many years, "if we would only apply to it all the common-sense things we know about how the members of our own families grow and develop strength!" The trouble is that we so often forget that Indians are people, too; that like ourselves all along the way to adulthood they must have experiences that lead to the next step in their growth. We know that, if our parents make all our important decisions for us, we are unhappy and fail to become independent adults. Yet that is what has happened to Indians for generations. They have been treated as if they were children, unable to decide things for themselves. When shall we begin to use common sense to help them solve their problems?

Indian Americans only want and need the same things that people of other races do. They want the right to work. They want equality of opportunity. They want political and social freedom. They have never asked to be relieved of responsibility, nor are they asking for that now. They want the chance to carry their own burdens and to make their own mistakes. If equal opportunity is denied them, they do not suffer alone. The malnourished Indian boy who comes to your city for work is a

menace to the whole community because of his suscepti-
bility to disease. The Indian farm land where erosion
remains unchecked threatens with equal danger the
white neighbor's land across the pasture fence. The Indian reservation beaten down by poverty and its attendant evils pulls down the level of well-being of the whole
state and nation.

Nor does the Indian alone profit when he is given educational opportunities and leadership responsibilities.
Where workers are needed, the trained Indian is ready
to do his part. From Indian homes and schools where
the lore of the tribe and techniques of healthful, constructive living in a modern world have been taught,
come the kind of citizens that America needs today.
Churches that interpret the Christian way of life to Indians are helping to develop community leaders for any
situation that may come in the future.

Indian welfare and happiness, Indian needs and perils,
are interdependent with your life and mine—for *Indians
are people, too.*

A SELECTED READING LIST

The following books and pamphlets have been selected from many written about the life of Indian Americans to offer suggestions to young people and leaders of youth who are planning local church programs, who desire books for reference use by study groups, or who wish to recommend books for reading by young people in their teens. Other books are listed on pages 168-173 of *The Indian in American Life*, by G. E. E. Lindquist.

PROGRAM MATERIAL

"Discussion and Program Suggestions for Seniors on the American Indian," by John D. Banks. New York, Friendship Press, 1944. 25 cents.

"This Is the Indian," by Earle F. Dexter. New York, Friendship Press, 1944. 25 cents. A pictorial book.

"What Kind of Democracy Do You Want?" by D. Campbell Wyckoff. New York, Friendship Press, 1944. 25 cents. A guide for young people studying Indians as a test case for American democracy.

REFERENCE BOOKS

American Indians and Their Music, by Frances Densmore. New York, Woman's Press, 1926. $1.00. History, customs, and music.

Book of Indian Crafts and Indian Lore, by Julian H. Salomon. New York, Harper & Brothers, 1928. $3.50.

Changing Indian, The, edited by Oliver La Farge. Norman,

Oklahoma, University of Oklahoma Press, 1942. $2.00. A symposium on the present status of the Indian.

Indian How Book, The, by Arthur C. Parker. Garden City, Doubleday, Doran & Co., 1927. $2.50. Indian life in camp and on the trail described by an Indian.

Indian in American Life, The, by G. E. E. Lindquist and collaborators. New York, Friendship Press, 1944. Cloth $1.00; paper 60 cents. An interpretation of Indian peoples with special emphasis upon their religious life and their future.

"Indian Wardship." New York, Home Missions Council, 1943. 15 cents. A study of the implications of wardship.

Indians of the United States, by Clark Wissler. Garden City, Doubleday, Doran & Co., 1941. $3.75. A description of how Indians live today, of their contributions to American culture, and of their rôle in America's future.

Speaking of Indians, by Ella C. Deloria. New York, Friendship Press, 1944. Cloth $1.00; paper 60 cents. A readable interpretation of some of the deeper experiences of Indians.

Twentieth Century Indians, by Frances Cooke Macgregor. New York, G. P. Putnam's Sons, 1941. $3.00. A survey of the life of modern Indians, with excellent photographs.

We Called Them Indians, by Flora Warren Seymour. New York, D. Appleton-Century Co., 1940. $2.00. A brief history of the Indians of the United States.

BOOKS FOR READING

American: The Life Story of a Great Indian, by Frank B. Linderman. New York, The John Day Co., 1930. $3.50. The life of Plenty-coups, Chief of the Crows.

Crazy Weather, by Charles L. McNichols. New York, The Macmillan Co., 1944. $2.00. A white boy's adventures in the Indian country.

First Penthouse Dwellers of America, by Ruth Underhill.

New York, J. J. Augustin, 1938. $2.75. Authentic portrayal of Pueblo Indian life.

Last Frontier, The, by Howard M. Fast. New York, Duell, Sloan & Pearce, 1941. $2.50. The tragedy of the Cheyenne trek to the Black Hills in 1870.

Legends of the Mighty Sioux, The, compiled by workers of the South Dakota Writers' Project, Work Projects Administration. Chicago, Albert Whitman & Company, 1941. $1.50.

Man Who Killed the Deer, The, by Frank Waters. New York, Farrar & Rinehart, Inc., 1942. $2.50. A Pueblo student discovers differences between Indian ways and white ways.

Mesa Land, by Anna Wilmarth Ickes. Boston, Houghton Mifflin Co., 1933. $3.00. Romance of Indian life in the Southwest.

Narcissa Whitman, Pioneer of Oregon, by Jeanette Eaton. New York, Harcourt, Brace & Co., 1941. $2.50. The adventures of a pioneer missionary.

People on the Earth, by Edwin Corle. New York, Random House, Inc., 1937. $2.00. A novel portraying the school and reservation life of a Navajo boy.

Ramona, by Helen Hunt Jackson. Boston, Little, Brown & Co., 1939. $1.50. Indian life in old California.

Sacajawea of the Shoshones, by Della Gould Emmons. Portland, Oregon, Binfords & Mort, 1943. $2.50. A novel.

Shadow over Wide Ruin, by Florence Crannell Means. Boston, Houghton Mifflin Co., 1942. $2.00. A Navajo story.

Son of the First People, A, by Adelaide W. Arnold. New York, The Macmillan Co., 1940. $2.00. Indian life today.

Waterless Mountain, by Laura Adams Armer. New York, Longmans, Green & Co., 1931. $2.50. Details of Navajo customs and tribal beliefs.

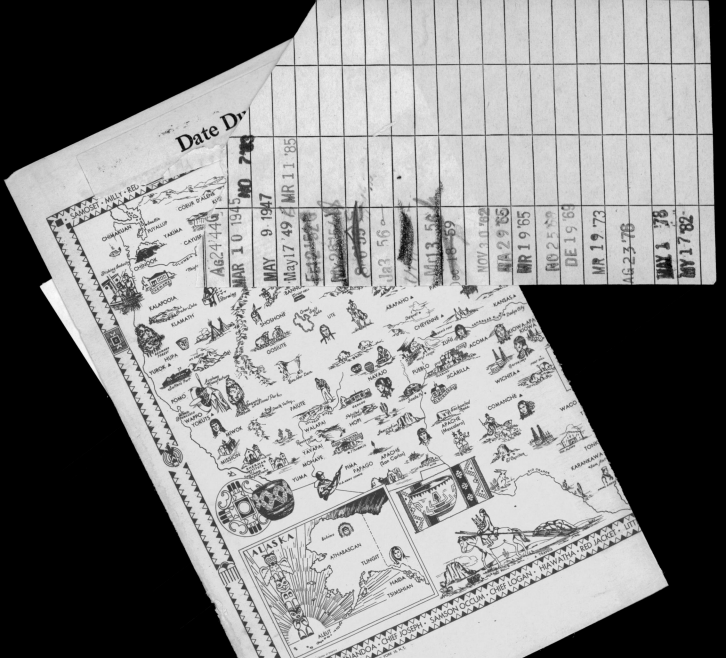